THE
FOOD
FORWARD
GARDEN

THE FOOD FORWARD GARDEN

A Complete Guide to Designing and Growing Edible Landscapes

CHRISTIAN DOUGLAS

Foreword by Tyler Florence

Artisan | New York

For Bonnie and Rosie

Library of Congress Cataloging-in-Publication Data is on file.

ISBN 978-1-64829-154-8

Interior design by Toni Tajima
Cover design by Rodrigo Corral

Artisan books may be purchased in bulk for business, educational,
or promotional use. For information, please contact your local
bookseller or the Hachette Book Group Special Markets
Department at special.markets@hbgusa.com.

The publisher is not responsible for websites (or their content) that
are not owned by the publisher.

The Hachette Speakers Bureau provides a wide
range of authors for speaking events. To find out
more, go to hachettespeakersbureau.com or email
HachetteSpeakers@hbgusa.com.

Published by Artisan,
an imprint of Workman Publishing,
a division of Hachette Book Group, Inc.
1290 Avenue of the Americas
New York, NY 10104
artisanbooks.com

The Artisan name and logo are registered trademarks of
Hachette Book Group, Inc.

Printed in China on responsibly sourced paper
First printing, September 2024

10 9 8 7 6 5 4 3 2 1

Contents

Foreword

EVERY SO OFTEN, IF YOU'RE LUCKY, you come across a person who becomes a true collaborator on your creative journey. Someone who not only has a passion and vision in their own field that matches yours, but someone who is able to create something alongside you that is greater than the sum of your individual parts. For me, that person is Christian Douglas. And that something is my chef's garden.

When my family moved into our 1890s-era Bernard Maybeck home in the spring of 2014, there was plenty of work to be done. But my wife, Tolan, and I were mostly focused on the landscaping. Tolan imagined a beautiful English-style garden to match the architecture of the house, but with an overgrown 7-acre (2.8 ha) plot, we needed help with our vision.

We found Christian, who convinced us that a stone and willow multitiered chef's garden, steps away from the kitchen, should be our priority. Who was I to argue? We started to dig, and six months later, the seeds were planted.

Christian isn't just a guy with a green thumb; he's a true artist. Every plot he designs is a one-of-a-kind, signature concept; a visionary botanical space that's a seamless blend of structure and nature. He has an amazing ability to tell stories through the outdoor worlds he creates.

He's also—and this was of the utmost importance to me—someone who cares deeply about food. It's a central theme in this book: the idea that growing food close to where we live, and making it look beautiful, is something we should all be striving to emulate. Certainly, in our garden, that's the case. At any given point in the year, we might have anything from lemongrass to lovage, artichokes that flower between ferns, or the sweetest summer tomatoes. He always makes sure to devote a section of real estate to chiles, so that I can make the fourteen-day lacto-fermented hot sauce that I give away as Christmas gifts every year.

As the garden has bloomed, so has our friendship. This has been the most fun collaboration for both of us, and I truly believe that he has made my food better, allowing me the opportunity to have impeccable ingredients on hand whether I'm shooting cookbooks, filming for television, or hosting intimate dinners at the house where guests can snack their way through the garden during cocktail hour.

He has also given me pearls of wisdom that you'll find throughout this book. You'll read about tending soil to increase nutrient density and heighten flavor. You'll find tips for choosing plants, growing food in any season, and designing spaces that feel both personal and practical. It's a template and a manual as much as it's a delight to flip through.

I'm so thrilled that the world can now benefit from his great work. I trust that the Christian Douglas touch is soon to find its way into your backyard. There's simply nothing better.

—TYLER FLORENCE

Introduction

IN A LAND FAR, FAR AWAY . . . you'll often find the vegetable garden. Commonly nestled behind fences or wedged into shady corners, edible plants are so often an afterthought rather than an asset. What if, instead, we brought food *forward*—out of the shadows and into our landscapes in a way that highlights these plants' beauty and seasonal offerings? What if we embraced vegetables, fruits, herbs, and berries, letting them share the prime real estate in our yards alongside our patios, pools, even our front walk? As gardeners, we have the potential to reimagine and redefine the ornamental landscape, to feed our neighborhoods—to create a new normal. By learning how to integrate food into our outdoor spaces, we can make better use of our time and resources without sacrificing style. Let me show you how to blend beauty and function and bring more purpose and meaning to the everyday garden.

Growing up in the south of England, I was exposed to gardens both modest and grand. My father, an original postwar victory gardener, grew food in an allotment, where I spent many evenings after school alongside him planting, pruning, and harvesting. Pulling up carrots and unearthing potatoes were my favorite "chores," and I fondly remember going over to the rusty tap, washing the dirt off a carrot, and sinking my teeth in. It was love at first bite.

After studying landscape design and horticulture, I became a partner at a design and fine gardening company, helping to create landscapes on magnificent, historic country estates and behind London townhomes. I was deeply enamored with the craftsmanship and details of these storied grounds, seduced by the herbaceous borders, walled kitchen gardens, old orchards, chalk streams, and wildflower meadows that surrounded them. There was never a dull moment—my partners and I went on to win awards at the Chelsea Flower Show, operate a private garden-tour company, and open an antique shop in Kensington. Through that decade, I grew to understand the transportive, whimsical joy that gardens deliver through the seasons. This was the stuff of classic tales. But, as with all good stories, there was another lesson to learn.

I began to wonder, with all of the effort and attention we give to our ornamental landscapes, could they be doing more? And so I departed my native soil in search of answers, setting off on a multiyear self-study of our relationship to the greater landscape that would ultimately bring me back to garden design in a more purposeful way.

Driven by my piqued curiosity, I wanted to observe firsthand how populations and cultures have lived off the land for thousands of years in challenging environments. I dug in deep, working with local communities and nonprofit organizations, on my own and with seasoned masters in the fields of regenerative agriculture, permaculture, and natural building processes. Again and again, from the mesquite Sonoran deserts of the American Southwest and the finger lime hinterlands of Australia to the buckthorn reaches of the rocky Himalayas and the salted soils and date palms of the Dead Sea valley, I saw a reverence for the natural world and an understanding of how careful land stewardship is essential to both our personal survival and that of our crops. I witnessed multigenerational families growing food and medicine together, passing ecological literacy down through the branches of their ancestral trees.

Landscapes are, and have always been, a resource. A place of nourishment and refuge. A way to sustain life and create resiliency. With today's environmental uncertainty and the rising need for local access to healthy food, now, more than ever, is the time to lean into those strengths. Where once the great British garden designers Gertrude Jekyll and Capability Brown had been my idols, local farmers and land stewards were now my inspiration.

The obvious question then became: Why were more people not growing food in their own gardens? The truth is, farming and landscape design aren't the most obvious bedfellows. They are both rooted in the same things—plants and soil, water and seasons, planning and patience—but often exist at cross purposes. After all, farming is intrinsically tied to efficient productive output, while modern-day design is principally focused on beauty and recreation. Combining the two would be a challenge, yet that's what interested me most, as a matchmaker with experience in both fields.

So my pursuit of food forward design began. I set up a business to explore whether prevailing design sensibilities could play nicely with food. I assembled a wonderful team of professional farmers, designers, and landscape architects to not only design and install edible landscapes and infrastructure but also mentor and educate other home farmers, all with the goal of making our neighborhoods more nutritious and creating spaces where plant knowledge can grow from one generation to the next.

Together over the past twelve years, we have found that the design itself plays a significant role in the ongoing success of growing food. You've heard the saying "We eat with our eyes"; well, we garden with them, too. When the garden is brought closer to the home, the family visits more frequently, learns faster, increases yields, eats healthier, and shares more with family and friends. And when the food is nearby, curb appeal counts: If we walk past our garden five times a day, entertain guests nearby, or gaze at it while doing the dishes, we want the area to look beautiful and feel cohesive with the surroundings.

All gardens, no matter their size, shape, or location, have the potential to transform our lives if we allow them. And there's no better way to do so than by including food in the process. After all, what other plants have the power to sustain, nurture, heal, and delight all five senses at once? Being a gardener is a continual learning experience, a collaboration between you and nature that is always evolving. When you start to look at your garden through a food forward lens, the edible opportunities are endless. I encourage you to explore the possibilities with an open mind and a healthy appetite. After that first harvest, I'm confident you'll fall in love, too.

How to Use This Book

This is a guidebook—part inspiration, part instruction—designed to gently steer you toward including more food in your landscape and daily life. My aim is to help you, dear reader, discover new ways to think outside the vegetable box and experiment with using a wide range of edible species to create beautiful and delicious outdoor spaces.

Start with the Principles of Food Forward Design. These ten tenets are at the heart of every project I create, and designed to help you integrate and maintain edible plants in your own garden.

Part I takes you on a tour through eight exemplary landscapes. From small city lots to larger country properties, from formal English arrangements to low-water habitats, each garden is designed with food top of mind. Following each garden tour is a spotlight on a particular facet of food forward gardening, including trellising, container planting, and cultivating native edibles.

Part II highlights a few unexpected but nonetheless promising places to grow food: rooftops, meadows, front yards, and even the forest floor. Despite each one's unique set of challenges, there are helpful pointers to ensure your success in similar situations.

Part III is the hardworking section, rife with design theory and practical hands-on advice from our team of farmers. We break down the most oft-repeated terms you will hear as you begin building healthy soil; planting and growing your own fruits, herbs, and vegetables; and (the fun part) harvesting and eating your homegrown bounty. A few clever craft projects follow, so that you may beautifully show off the fruits of your labor. And finally, we include a primer on the garden tools and equipment we love most.

Part IV is a comprehensive guide to our favorite edible plants, flowers, and pollinator species. I hope it inspires you to introduce more edible powerhouses into your landscape.

Finally, the send-off: the Plant Index. This serves as a quick reference to a deeper bench of diverse—and tasty—varieties, broken down by harvest time, climate zone, and sun requirements, to ensure you'll have something delicious to eat whenever and wherever you are.

The Principles of
Food Forward Design

1 **Plant in Plain Sight.** Grow food close to the house, where you're
bound to see it. The nearer edibles are to high-traffic areas, the
more frequently you will tend to them, the better they will look, and
the more often you will harvest them.

2 **Start Small.** To avoid overwhelm, keep your garden plan simple
at the outset. Plant just a few edibles, in amounts that your own
household can comfortably consume, and add more as your confidence
grows.

3 **Blend Botanicals.** Edible varieties and ornamental species are
not mutually exclusive. If fact, the two can—and should—coexist
harmoniously. Practice pairing them together in the same planting bed.

4 **Think Beyond Vegetables.** Include fruits, berries, herbs, and
edible flowers in your planting plan, too, and you'll be opening
the door to more interesting and diverse menus.

5 **Plan Ahead.** When devising your planting scheme, aim to stagger
the harvest with plants that flower and fruit at different times of
the year so there is something to admire and feast on throughout the
seasons.

6 **Invite Garden Guests.** Pollination powers food production. Be sure to include at least one water feature and plenty of flowering plants that attract and nourish bees and other pollinators.

7 **Share the Sun.** The sunniest areas—commonly reserved for dining terraces, outdoor kitchens, and pools—are also prime territory for growing food. Get creative with how you integrate the two.

8 **Elevate the Space.** Materials define a garden as much as plant life, so invest in quality fixtures, fittings, and furnishings. Artwork, including sculpture and statuary, creates focal points that draw you into the garden and enhance the food-growing experience.

9 **Engage Often.** The more time you spend interacting with the garden, the more you will learn from it. Attending to tasks in regular, small doses should keep maintenance from feeling like a chore.

10 **Take a Seat.** Integrate seating into your main food-growing areas to encourage frequent (and lengthy) stays. Give yourself the opportunity to slow down, relax, and breathe deeply among the birds, butterflies, and bees.

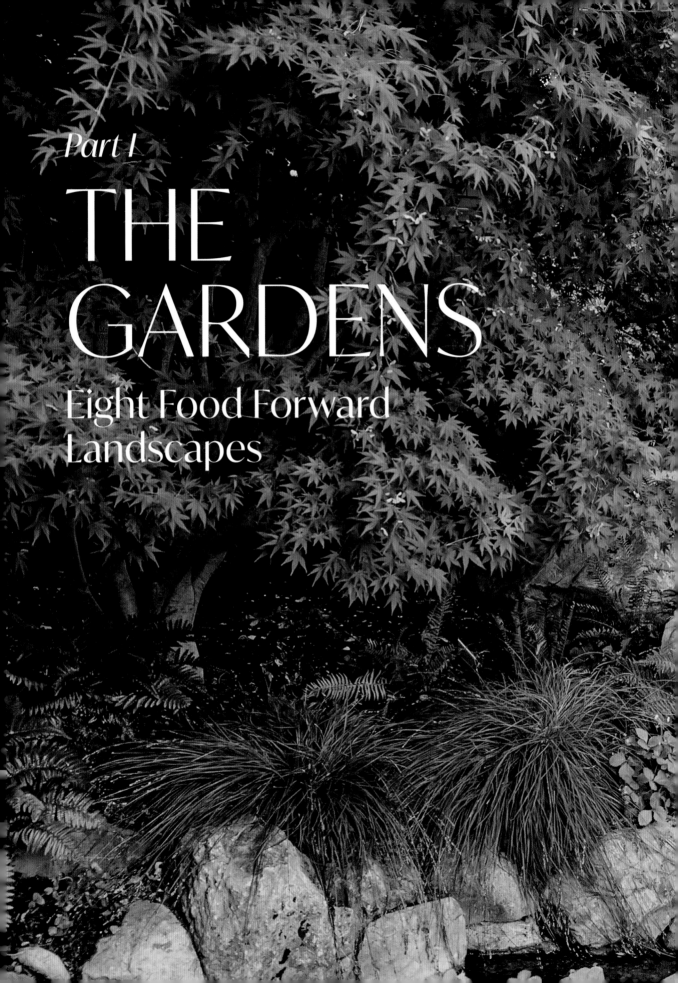

Part I

THE GARDENS

Eight Food Forward Landscapes

IN MY EXPERIENCE, THE BEST WAY TO ENCOURAGE people to grow their own food is to lead by example. The eight gardens profiled in this chapter, featuring edible landscapes in a range of locations and styles, are designed to do just that. There's no single formula for growing food, nor a one-size-fits-all template to follow. That's a big part of what keeps it so interesting and ultimately rewarding for me. Food forward gardens can thrive in rural, suburban, and metropolitan settings, and everywhere in between. In the pages that follow, you'll see plots of all shapes and sizes that suit different microclimates, lifestyles, and plant palette (and palate) preferences, along with advice and tips to help you grow an edible oasis all your own.

HOMESTEAD HARVEST

THE PATH FROM THE CITY TO THE SUBURBS is a familiar one, and well trodden by many would-be gardeners with young children in tow. In this case, the homeowners dreamed of transforming an unremarkable lot into a somewhat wild and wonder-filled playground, a place where their two adventurous boys could roam and play while surrounded on all sides by homegrown treats. Together, we hatched a plan inspired by the homeowners' dream of foraging for food. In the process, we transformed the existing landscape, which felt sterile, into a richly layered, cohesive, wraparound space. The result is a thriving habitat of fruit trees, berry bushes, edible flowers, and herbal ground cover, each offering ongoing nourishment, visual delights, and engagement opportunities for its many occupants—adults, kids, animals, and insects alike.

These days, wandering and discovery are encouraged at every corner. Multiple water features help set the tone and invite much-needed pollinators to the party. We introduced a meandering stream through the formerly vacant side yard, where the children now spend endless hours searching for berries and newts. Elsewhere, their parents plan meals with whichever vegetables are in season and gather fruit from the trees. The more they experiment with planting and harvesting, the more curious they are to learn about growing more food. All in all, the design goes to show that when you put the right structure in place and let nature have its way, there's no such thing as going astray.

Only a Step Away

Just beyond the kitchen door lie abundant layers of culinary herbs, citrus, blueberries, and vegetables. A crabapple tree holds sway above the retaining walls, creating a soft, defused separation between the dining terrace and pool below.

Shared Space

A series of stacked redwood-beam raised beds shares the
sunshine with the pool—a prime example of food production
coexisting beautifully with high-traffic spaces. Anchored into
the house's low stone perimeter, the planter beds become a
seamless extension of the building itself.

Creekside →

The secluded rocky stream and rustic plank bridges quickly became a favorite place to play, where the kids forage for alpine strawberries and huckleberries while maneuvering toy trucks through the understory.

Pie in the Sky ↘

A prolific 'Wynoochee Early' apple tree is espaliered against the south-facing wall of the house, extending the food production skyward.

Red-handed ↓

Strawberry plants are dotted throughout the site, planted along low walls and taller ledges so that their bright berries dangle over the edges, ensuring the fruit is easy to spot and less accessible to pests.

Garden Portal → →

The rusted-steel moon gate, flanked by pineapple guava and 'Pakistan' mulberries, marks the threshold between the sunny backyard and the shady side yard.

← ← Hens and Hives

Busy beehives are tucked in next to figs and artichokes. Honey is harvested once or twice per year, keeping the family well stocked with sweetener throughout the seasons. With white framing and finials to match those on the house, the chicken coop is dedicated to rescue hens that turn food scraps and garden green waste into nutritious eggs.

← Warm Welcome

Inside the gate, everbearing strawberries encircle a converted sugar kettle fountain set in a courtyard of apple trees, lavender, artichokes, and *Pennisetum* grasses.

↓ Street Food

Four varieties of table grapes face the street and 'Mission' fig trees frame the entryway, inviting neighbors to stop for a bite as they pass by.

Hiding in Plain Sight

This backyard landscape may appear purely ornamental, but it is also surprisingly fruitful. Dwarf 'Bonfire' peach trees make a bold match for red Abyssinian bananas (in the foreground), while thyme, marjoram, and oregano weave through the stepping stones. Beyond, 'Arctic Supreme' peach, 'Fuyu' persimmon, 'Bearss' lime, 'Eureka' lemon, and 'Nagami' kumquat trees blend into borders, producing bushels of fruit all year long.

WATER FEATURES

When we focus our gardening efforts on edible plantings, we quickly become more aware of our reliance on bees and other pollinator species, without whom most flowers would never produce fruit. Our natural surroundings are also infinitely more memorable, and sustainable, when they attract frequent visitors—birds, bees, and beyond. Flowers look that much brighter when butterflies abound, and a landscape truly comes alive with the thrum of hummingbirds.

To support the thriving industry of these garden visitors, include at least one water source in your landscape. In addition to welcoming wildlife, it will provide ambience, movement, and sound to your outdoor space. As with all garden accessorizing, you want the feature to fit within the context and spirit of the landscape, so choose wisely.

The Details

Function Standing fountains with dry edges allow birds to rest in place while they sip. Shallow gradient edges create space for bees and smaller-legged friends to sidle up and rehydrate without risk of drowning. If you have a deeper pond, consider adding a large rock to create a dry "island" for pollinators to recharge. (Note: The size of your water feature is not as important as its accessibility. Pollinators have an innate ability to source water supplies, no matter how small.)

Style The beauty of water features is that almost anything can be turned into one, so you have some creative license. Even a small bubbling bowl offers enough to keep the community going. Stone troughs, rills, and steel sugar kettles each bring a timeless formality, whereas streams and pools nestle nicely into a natural setting.

Location Shady locations are ideal for water features because evaporation steals water quickly from full-sun sites throughout the summer months. The next best location is one with morning sun only.

❶ A Corten steel waterfall feature amplifies this custom creek with rocky pools designed for wildlife. ❷ Birdbaths are simple, inexpensive, and timeless. ❸ A trickling water wall provides convenient ledges for thirsty visitors. ❹ Of the many variations on bubbling fountains, this shallow, gently dripping millstone is ideal for thirsty insects.

COUNTRY COTTAGE

FROM THE OUTSET, the owner of this charming wine-country property saw the potential for life-changing magic in the underused garden. Having access to freshly picked, all-natural ingredients, she reasoned, might help her stick to a plant-based diet of mostly home-cooked meals.

Thankfully, the lot that surrounds the home is blessed with plenty of sunlight. The only trick? Exercising restraint. By carving out clearly defined seating areas, keeping planting beds slim, and maintaining flow from each area to the next, we were able to create a well-proportioned garden that is filled to the brim with food yet never feels overwhelming. It's important to keep the scale in line not only with the garden size but with the stamina of the budding gardener as well.

Now, a few small steps from the kitchen door to the garden yields substantial returns toward the homeowner's goals. High-frequency harvest crops (leafy greens, peas, herbs, and strawberries, among others) are planted in a series of geometric beds, fruit trees (figs, apples, citrus) border the pool, and the arches spanning the pathways support climbing squashes and gourds. The seasons bring fluctuations in the landscape as the owner's priorities shift. Some years, she grows more edible plants, and others, a greater number of flowers for cutting and arranging. The result is an edible landscape that doubles as a catalyst for learning new skills and adopting healthier habits.

Sidelined No More

An awkward side yard, too often a repository for junk in residential landscapes, offers a place to grow food and flowers in large-format planters. While not as visible from within the house as the main potager, this lot makes the perfect setting for the more boisterous plants to run and climb with abandon.

Lush Geometry

Through the tasteful arrangement of elements, inspired by formal French potagers, this eye-catching kitchen garden holds its own in the central location of the yard. The four L-shaped beds made of stacked redwood beams are accessible from all sides and at a comfortable height for harvesting.

Private Dining ↑

Placing a table just inside the front gate sets the tone of relaxed hospitality that pervades the rest of the property. Thanks to the dense hedge of culinary bay and tall fruiting olive trees screening the road and neighboring houses, the front yard feels surprisingly private.

Supporting Cast →

The beam-and-wire arbors that span the narrow side yard support an array of rambunctious cucumbers, beans, peas, summer squash, winter squash, tomatoes, and cutting roses. The raised beds below are home to a rotating ensemble of staple crops such as potatoes, onions, and garlic.

← ← Potager Pairing

Growing space is maximized by planting perennial strawberries, herbs, and edible flowers (such as sweet alyssum and violas) around the perimeter, with vegetables (including 'Breen' lettuces, 'Diva' cucumbers, and 'Fairytale' eggplants) packed in at close quarters.

← Berries and Blooms

Sweet 'Sunshine' blueberries and scented 'Hidcote' lavender pair nicely in the perennial border.

↙ Gold Standard

As with most zucchini, this 'Gold Rush' variety is so prolific it seems to double in size almost overnight, brightening up any summer garden or salad.

↓ New Heights

One of the few vining summer squash that can easily race up and over even the tallest archway, this unique 'Centercut' variety boasts a distinctive sweet and nutty flavor.

The Sun and Stars

Espaliered 'Fuji' apples adorn the fence behind the firepit, creating a green backdrop and architectural symmetry for the view across the pool. They also produce bushels of fruit each fall. An open-top timber pergola frames the space, offering a sense of seclusion while still allowing late-night stargazing.

Fruitful Shade

Beyond the pool, mature 'Mission' fig and 'Eureka' lemon trees provide prodigious amounts of produce and double as welcome sunshades all summer long. The trees are underplanted with globes of 'Little Ollie' dwarf olive, blueberries, gardenia, and Euphorbia 'Shorty' for a classically calming combination of green and white.

TRELLISING

Vertical space is untapped garden real estate. Putting it to use is an easy, effective way to increase your harvest without expanding your garden's footprint. Planting vertically also allows you to establish new layers and points of interest, interrupting the monotony of the ground plane. An excellent study in form and function, trellising lends great style to the landscape as it provides sturdy support for a variety of fruiting perennials and annual vegetables.

Before choosing your structure, consider the mature size of the plants you want to grow. Some species can dominate even a robust climbing tower (a single male kiwifruit, for example, can grow 20 feet/6.1 m high). In the case of vigorous vines (such as grapes, kiwi, passion fruit, hops, and thornless blackberries), opt for stable, durable trellises such as pergolas, archways, or walls. Many vegetables, while not as imposing, can reach more than 6 feet (1.8 m) tall, so providing a vertical framework may be necessary to keep the plants healthy. The benefits are many: increasing sun exposure, reducing the chances of broken branches or disease, and lessening pest issues caused by contact with the damp ground. Because garden beds are ever-evolving seasonal spaces, I lean toward movable and even storable structures for annual plants—among them squashes, gourds (including pumpkins), tomatoes, cucumbers, melons, peas, beans, and Malabar spinach. Many of these climbers flower before fruiting (peas and scarlet runners have especially pretty blooms), adding a nice bit of adornment to the structure.

The Options

Obelisk Much more elegant than the common (and flimsy) wire tomato cages, obelisks can be constructed of metal, willow, or wood. Typically, we use 5-foot-tall (1.5 m) obelisks. The square shape and open center of a simple iron structure lends itself to large branching plants (think tomatoes), whereas more intricate or circular obelisks with narrow tops favor vining plants (like peas and beans).

Bamboo Tower An affordable construction of bamboo and pins, these expandable structures have three sides and are perfect for smaller vining plants including peas, pole beans, and cucumbers.

Archway If you have the room for an archway spanning two beds, don't hesitate to install one. These structures provide highly productive growing space all while posing as stylized transition points

In addition to providing scaffolding for plants (like the Malabar spinach pictured here), this cedar obelisk adds statuesque interest to the garden bed.

through the landscape. There is nothing quite like the satisfaction of walking through a green tunnel dripping with fresh produce. Mark each season with something new growing up and over the archway: sweet pea flowers, pumpkins, peas, or cherry tomatoes, for example.

Flat Panel Where space is particularly tight, or when growing against a wall or fence, flat trellises are a wise choice. Metal ones are available in a wide variety of styles, including galvanized, powder-coated, and rusted. A simple wood lattice is another dependable option.

A-Frame Wooden posts or bamboo poles can be used to fashion an inexpensive, sturdy, tepee-shaped structure, secured at the top with twine.

Espalier This popular technique involves training a plant flat against a surface, either a solid wall or fence or a free-standing frame with cables. In addition to screening fence lines, espaliered trees add strong architectural detail to a landscape; even during winter (when branches are leafless), a tree's structure maintains its inherent beauty. Espalier is also a practical way to camouflage fence lines (as in the photo on page 40): The greenery softens the edges of a yard, making it feel more spacious, less hemmed in.

Pergola These solidly built wood or metal structures create practical, largely covered areas within a garden (or offer entry to it). They also serve as focal points, with rambling vines and climbers only increasing their romantic charm. Larger perennials like kiwifruit and grapes will take some years to get established on this type of trellising, but because they are deciduous plants, once mature they will provide shade during summer and allow sunlight through in winter after they lose their leaves.

❶ Patinated hogwire arches support 'Flame' table grape vines and turn an ordinary pathway into a foraging tunnel. ❷ This simple A-frame trellis is well suited for annual vegetables in rectangular beds. ❸ Espalier pears, if within arm's reach, are a perfect pick for narrow spaces.

CITY LIFE

GROWING FOOD IN THE CITY presents more than its fair share of challenges, thanks largely to the inevitable limitations on space and light. Nevertheless, many city gardeners remain determined in their pursuit. They expect a lot of whatever space is available to them (and rightly so), trying to eke out as much as they can from small exterior footprints. Urban landscaping, then, calls for ingenuity, clever engineering, and carefully stacked priorities.

This town house near the ocean's edge in San Francisco proved no exception to the rule. The owners wanted to maximize space for an edible garden, without sacrificing room for entertaining friends and relaxing on days off. For economy of space, we began by creating a series of boxes within boxes, utilizing vertical planes and leaning heavily into a combination of considered materials and design details, including plantings for all seasons. After all, each decision weighs more heavily in such a small footprint, where no element goes unnoticed. From a food forward perspective, the focus in an urban setting is often on supplemental plants rather than sustenance, seasonal accents and flavor boosters (herbs, cherry tomatoes, citrus) over larger, production-scale crops. The payouts are different than in larger residential gardens, but considerable nonetheless. Just having a few homegrown ingredients on hand at the end of a long day, saving yourself a trip to the store, helps slow the nonstop pace of city living.

Social Settings

This small city lot boasts an upper-deck dining area with room to grill, a day bed for napping beneath the rose-covered trellis, and a central open space for larger gatherings.

Blurred Boundaries

Framing recreation spaces with raised planting beds helps soften the edges, creating a lush, layered backdrop. All the better if those beds offer something you can nibble on! This yard is bordered with six citrus trees, two espaliered apple trees, and several blueberry bushes nestled into stone planters.

← Sweet and Sour

Tart kumquats underplanted with alpine strawberries flank the studio doors. Along the perimeter, pink foxgloves and purple 'Rozanne' geraniums add color to the verdant ensemble of ferns, oakleaf hydrangeas, boxwoods, rosemary, and magnolia trees.

↑ Simple Greens

Two lumber planters are notched into the surrounding stone walls. The change of material highlights the small but mighty vegetable garden. Because space is limited, fast-growing produce—such as kale and salad greens—is prioritized.

← Herb Appeal

Basil, oregano, parsley, cilantro, and the like are incorporated into daily meals while mint and lemon balm add fragrance and flavor to morning teas.

↑ Cocktail Hour

Directly outside the kitchen door, sleek black metal herb pots, a stocked bar cart, and a dining table combine to make the perfect setup for easy drinks-to-dinner hosting.

Green Screening

This landscape is full of surprises, including the work-from-home studio that easily transforms into a backdrop for movie nights. The arrangement encourages spending more time *en plein air*, beneath the stars and immersed in the plants.

CONTAINER GARDENS

Pots and planters offer (nearly) endless options for cultivating an edible garden, in materials and styles to fit any space, regardless of square footage or budget. They also provide an opportunity for contrasting textures and colors to work with your decorating scheme, including your home's exterior. Keep variations in check, however, and play with planter sizes within a narrow color palette for a more unified look.

The Details

Size Large rectangular planters work well for annual vegetables, re-creating the feel and organization of a mini raised bed, with plenty of room for all the roots (aim for a minimum depth of 1 foot/30.5 cm). Deep round pots (at least 2 feet/0.6 m deep) are just right for dwarf fruit trees and berry bushes, as well as for individually planted annual vegetables, such as tomatoes and eggplants. Smaller vessels are best suited to herbs and leafy greens.

Watering Pots and smaller planters dry out faster than larger planting beds, meaning more frequent watering. This is especially true for porous materials, which lose more to evaporation, as well as for metal vessels, which can heat up quickly in the sun (though trailing greenery can act as a buffer).

On the flip side, pots with poor drainage will drown plants, so make sure water can drain freely. To avoid staining decks or patios, you can add a catch drain or tray under the planter.

Proximity If you have the space to install planters near a grill or outdoor cooktop, use them for herbs, edible flowers, and other flavor enhancers and garnishes that you'll want within easy reach.

Softened Edges Allowing strawberries or trailing flowers such as sweet alyssum, Bacopa, or nasturtium to hang over the edges of your pot adds beauty to any container scheme.

Planting Strategy Avoid mixing vigorous spreaders, such as mint and oregano, with other plants, as they'll steal nutrients and crowd out the root zone.

❶ Terra-cotta's warm, natural look pairs well with greenery of all kinds. ❷ Galvanized metal troughs are versatile, befitting farmhouse and modern styles and anything in between. ❸ Sleek, lightweight metal and fiberglass planters are perfect for decks and balconies. ❹ Glazed ceramic pots can introduce an elegant shine and pop of color.

CHEF'S GARDEN

THE GREATEST PLEASURE FOR A LANDSCAPE DESIGNER, arguably, is working with a home gardener who transforms what you've planted into something infinitely more appealing. When that person is a culinary master and the garden features an abundance of fresh produce, the partnership becomes an endless serving of ideas and inspiration.

Such is the case in the home garden of chef Tyler Florence and his wife, Tolan. Because their lives revolve around cooking and celebrating, the design is focused, unsurprisingly, on growing food close to their active kitchen and dining areas. A steep, ivy-covered bank directly behind the house was the most intuitive, if tricky, area for planting. Terraced landscape arrangements aren't complicated per se, but they require thoughtful engineering and strategic planting.

Because the Florences entertain all year round, it's especially important that the landscape is composed of equal parts bounty and beauty. Growing annual vegetables in such a central location, next to the main living quarters and outdoor dining terraces, means that each landscape element vies for attention in a competitive zone. From season to season, the garden serves as the backdrop for large group gatherings and small family dinners alike.

In every square foot, you sense the partnership between chef and gardener. Food is richly woven into an ecosystem that's at once purposeful and pleasing, stylish and sustaining. Flowers add hints of color as they connect with other ornamentals and edibles in the garden. Together, the mix of materials and plantings adds up to one gorgeously immovable feast.

Hog Heaven
Mazzy, the family pig, makes her way down the terraced kitchen garden, paying a visit to the source of her steady diet of tasty garden scraps.

Menu Planning

Each season's planting palette is sure to include new vegetable varieties for the chef's latest culinary projects. Crop rotation, cut flowers, and a degree of visual symmetry are also factored into each tier of the garden.

← Between the Lines

The hillside has been divided into accessible terraces with clear pathways that make working in the garden easy from both above and below. The upper level was preserved as a grassy orchard and a paddock for the family's chickens and small herd of goats.

↑ Spring Harvest

Silvery artichokes command the tricky slope between the kitchen garden and orchard, adding architectural grace and edible hearts all spring long. A mix of contrasting green 'Provider' and purple 'Velour' bush beans drape over the terrace edges for easy picking.

All Fired Up

A steady supply of hyperlocal produce fuels Tyler's easy approach to home cooking. Vegetables and herbs are quickly sizzled over the flame of a cauldron-style grill or make their way into sides and hearty salads. An assortment of hot chiles inspires new recipes for the chef's signature hot sauces and preserves.

Sharing the Bounty

At the foot of the garden, the brick terrace makes a fitting venue for entertaining. Tolan puts her celebrated styling talents to good use, mixing freshly cut flowers and other natural elements with her collection of linens and plateware to suit the occasion—and the season—at hand.

HILLSIDE PLANTING

Challenge or opportunity? In the garden, steep slopes are a bit of both, inviting us to stretch our creative muscles and put our engineering skills to rigorous test. In short order, what was once an unused area becomes a newly forged and productive plot of land.

The Details

Materials Since hillside gardens combine retaining walls and raised beds in one design, durability is especially important. For the longest life span, choose thick lumber (redwood or cedar), stone, or concrete for terrace walls and stairs, in a style that works well with your existing landscape. Lumber is the simplest to construct with, but the shortest lived (avoid pressure-treated wood near edibles). Most masonry finishes have a wonderful timeless look, while concrete and steel read more modern. Gravel is a good choice for simple (and affordable) pathways. You can always upgrade them later with stone.

Berms and Basins On steep slopes, this leveling technique is often used when planting orchard trees (it's less common for vegetables). Semicircle berms (mounds of soil) on the downhill side result in a level basin that allows water and nutrients to infiltrate more slowly and mitigates erosion.

Planting Strategy Steeper terraces can create longer shadows, depending on their orientation (ideally, east to west), so choose wisely when deciding what to plant where. A linear structure simplifies the planting arrangement: The tallest crops are planted on the uphill side of each bed, midsize plants in the middle, and short or trailing varieties hang over the front edges.

Access When planning your terraces, carving out clear steps and pathways is crucial for safety as well as styling. You want to ensure you can reach every part of the garden bed from above and below without bending over (aim for planting beds no wider than 4 feet/1.2 m). Steeper slopes (3:1 ratio) with walls in the 30- to 36-inch (77 to 92 cm) range allow you to garden at a comfortable countertop height (at least from one side). The trade-off is the need for more stairs and materials, but the longer-term result is a more comfortable garden experience.

To help new terraces fit in, choose materials and finishes that complement existing architecture. In this case, lumber beds have been painted with a low-VOC dark gray paint to match the house and modern board-form concrete walls.

Not every terrace level has to match; you can mix it up by switching materials. Here, castellated wooden beds contrast beautifully with native rock retaining walls. Other complementary materials include steel, finished concrete, brick, and stucco.

FRENCH
FORMAL

WHEN DESIGNING A VEGETABLE GARDEN on a good-size lot, the natural temptation is to go deep and wide and largely out of sight. In this well-appointed property, however, we broke from that convention. Rather than planting an oversize plot in the back forty, as is the common practice, we narrowed the aperture with a sequence of smaller, open garden "rooms" adjacent to the home's living spaces. Scale and sight lines are more harmonious this way, and the reimagined layout is more practical, too.

Because its placement is so close to the areas where people tend to gather, the potager needed to stand alone as a beautiful landscape feature, which we achieved largely with a strong, intentionally refined design. Throughout the garden, quality materials and finishes are elevated with elements like willow raised beds and an antique limestone fountain. In the full sun–exposed site, we shied away from excessive hardscape, instead softening the area with perennial edible plants eager to soak up the UVs. The result is both a consistent delivery of food and a natural cooling effect.

The generous lot size allows for plenty of dedicated space to grow flowers in addition to food. As the colors ebb and flow through their cycles, the profusion of ornamental plants in bloom provides a haven for pollinators. It's another exercise in layering, as natural textures and colors are juxtaposed with materials, within measure—all in keeping with the home's clean, gracefully restrained lines.

Keep It Close
The kitchen doors open directly to the vegetable garden and expansive outdoor dining area, making it easy to run out and pick ingredients for any meal. Thoughtful layering of ground-level and raised planting beds partitions the long slice of land into distinct spaces, without blocking the views.

Windfall in the Willows

Additional detailing in central, high-visibility areas is important. Despite their larger size, these handsome 6-by-4-foot (1.8 by 1.2 m) raised beds (housing frequently harvested vegetables like greens, radishes, and tomatoes) remain elegant thanks to the addition of willow wattle siding and wooden trim cap.

Ripe for the Picking →

'Albion' strawberries hang over the edge of each raised bed, impossible to resist as you walk along the central pathway to the pool.

Cruciferous Contrast ↘

The glaucous leaves of the 'Ruby Perfection' cabbage provide welcome color and texture to the sea of green foliage.

Sun Seekers ↓

Avocado trees bask in the sun below the herb garden, bearing fruit in midwinter.

Going Up → →

A profusion of perennial herbs— including thyme, chives, tarragon, sage, and oregano—surround strikingly tall artichoke plants, playing beautifully with the hierarchy of architectural shape and form.

High Design

The purposeful symmetry and subtle division of space in this landscape is accentuated by the sculptural boxwood globes, clipped lavender borders, and espalier pear frame. Brick edge accents continue along the pathways, acting as the cohesive visual thread among other material choices.

← ← Floral Approach

A formerly unused lawn along the driveway was reimagined as a raised-bed flower garden nestled between evergreen hedges. An antique iron table creates an element of surprise, and doubles as a convenient workstation for flower arranging.

← Good as New

A fresh coat of paint was all it took to revitalize a retired potting bench. The workstation now keeps tools and supplies organized and close at hand for regular and impromptu garden visits.

↙ Rock and Rill

A narrow water rill introduced along the wide stone pathway moves the eye forward and offers refreshment for the many thirsty bees, butterflies, and hummingbirds.

↓ Color Story

Zinnias, cosmos, and verbena collide in a profusion of pink and purple hues.

Flower Power

The formality of the layout and the classic cutting-rose and catmint border lends a timeless sophistication to the flower garden. Central raised beds are dedicated to ever-changing, delightful flower varieties, such as dahlias, zinnias, cosmos, scabiosas, and poppies.

RAISED BEDS

As the name makes clear, raised beds sit off the ground, allowing you to garden in a self-contained environment—a microclimate of sorts. Among their many benefits, the beds incorporate the best parts of growing in ground (a roomy root zone, uniform moisture retention) while eliminating the most persistent challenges (gophers and other predators, poor quality or contaminated soil, and invasive weeds). Raised beds offer the best shot at gardening success with bountiful harvests, especially in residential settings, because they allow for more control over the soil, the greatest determining factor in plant health. (For more on Healthy Soil, see page 181.)

The Details

Materials Raised beds add height, interest, and structure to the ground plane and offer a chance to highlight materials that complement or contrast with your surroundings. Wood, woven willow, stone, and steel are our go-to options for raised beds, depending on the garden narrative and the planting scheme within them.

Size Perhaps the biggest advantage of raised beds is in the ergonomics: Planting, weeding, and harvesting are much more comfortable and even enjoyable when you don't have to bend and strain your back. Consider the bed width and height, for optimal reach. You want to be able to access plants easily from either long side. Four feet (1.2 m) wide is the standard; any wider and reaching the center can be arduous. When installing a single-reach raised bed—against a fence or wall, for example—keep the width at 3 feet (0.9 m) or less. A height of 18 to 24 inches (46 to 61 cm) is best for plants of all sizes.

❶ The English cottage look is achieved by attaching panels of woven willow to a wooden bed. ❷ Classic redwood-lumber raised beds are given a top cap and exterior posts for added detail. ❸ Sturdy and versatile, weathered steel lends itself well to both crisp outlines and curved edges. ❹ Stone beds are an age-old choice with a wonderful handcrafted feel.

SUBURBAN SANCTUARY

THIS SMALL FAMILY HOME illustrates why I consider the suburbs the unsung heroes of edible gardening. These areas offer an opportunity to push back on conventional theories of where and how best to grow food, and at the same time encourage us to rethink traditional yards, the majority of which are blessed with ample space and access to sunlight.

Surrounded by an L-shaped plot, the modern raised ranch sits on a busy street. Its owners envisioned transforming their traditional landscape of hydrangeas and dogwood trees into a self-supporting, low-water, edible oasis. By swapping out plants, they hoped to supplement their weekly farmers' market hauls with homegrown fruits, vegetables, and herbs, and to encourage visits from beneficial wildlife.

Now, fresh produce graces the front, back, and side yards year-round. And because of regional drought conditions, we added a passive rainwater harvesting system to slow the roof water runoff into the landscape.

As much as the owners are intent on growing food, lifestyle considerations factor into the plan for just how much of it to plant, and how to do so efficiently. Their frequent travel schedule means that slower-growing perennial edibles (fruits, berries, and herbs) win out over more time-sensitive annual vegetables. Designing for one's individual needs this way helps ensure that none of the harvest goes to waste. In fact, there's no end to the good use these two resourceful gardeners have found for their homegrown output.

Sitting in Style

The highlight of this patio is the built-in seating area nestled against a series of raised planting beds with an espalier lemon-and-lime hedge. Dark purple basil borders the backrest, perfuming the air and offering a stunning contrast to the eye-catching orange and crimson pillows.

Salad Bar →

Constant successions of salad greens work well for a family on the go.

Grape Escape ↘

A 'Concord' grape vine smothers the seating arbor and creates welcome summer shade. The fruit is turned into jelly each fall.

Worth the Squeeze ↓

The overabundance of limes from the citrus hedge are harvested in batches, then juiced and frozen for year-round use in dressings and drinks.

Deer Proof

The front of this property gets plenty of deer traffic, so the focus is on attracting pollinators with predator-proof teucrium, gaura, and salvias rather than tender edibles. Tall lemon and fruiting olive trees succeed in their ability to outgrow the predators.

A Feast for the Senses

The intimate courtyard is at once colorful and calm, packed with fruit trees, berries, and pollinator flowers including echinacea, 'Terracotta' yarrow, 'May Night' salvia, and 'Otto Quast' lavender.

← Purple Haze

Opal basil and chocolate cosmos rim the small habitat pool, attracting friendly insects and birds to help pollinate the Meyer lemon hedge above.

↑ Potted Up

Glazed terra-cotta pots of various sizes house blueberries, aggressive spreading herbs (including mint), and a nice mix of succulents. With their light-reflecting sheen, vessels like these are especially compelling when juxtaposed with low-luster materials like matte wood and gravel.

EDIBLE SWAPS

I am under no illusion that every plant in a yard must be edible (I have a penchant for nonedibles, too), but even adding in one or two begins to make a difference. With a purposeful shift in thinking, you can see that hedges, statement trees, evergreen shrubs, and ground covers all offer tasty opportunities for food production. The trick is to find an edible match with similar characteristics that can fulfill the same role in the landscape. Once you start swapping out common garden ornamentals for edible varieties it can be difficult to know where to stop. Remember, flowers turn to fruit, so not only will you fill your basket at harvesttime, but you'll also enjoy the floriferous display weeks and months before.

The Options

Trees Japanese maples are easily substituted with any deciduous fruit tree (provided you have enough sun)—try apple, mulberry, pear, or quince. Each boasts distinct foliage as well as beautiful spring blossoms. With their large, glossy evergreen leaves, magnolias are commonly used as ornamental trees, but avocado and loquat trees have a similar look and could serve the same design function in the right climate. Similarly, a persimmon tree makes a fine replacement for dogwood or Catalpa.

Hedges and Topiary Rather than wrapping your property in unexciting hedging, create a fruitful or fragrant border by, for example, swapping a clipped boxwood for a compact blueberry. Other robust culinary hedges to explore include sweet bay, rosemary, buckthorn, pineapple guava, and citrus.

Vines and Climbers The same approach applies to arbors and other structures that support climbers and vines. Choose productive grapes, kiwifruit, or passion fruit, for instance, in place of nonedible jasmine, wisteria, or bougainvillea.

Ground Cover Thyme, strawberry, yerba buena, and lingonberry plants all work well as edible ground covers.

Where a magnolia grandiflora would traditionally have been selected in front of a Victorian home, we opted for a 'Fuyu' persimmon and 'Mission' fig, seen here showing off their broad canopies as they begin a glorious show of autumn color.

CLASSIC ELEGANCE

IN ANY LANDSCAPE DESIGN, when the balance of living elements and the narrative of the home is right, that push and pull creates dynamism and delight. When it's not, a shift is in order. Case in point: this property, which was marked by swaths of concrete and terra-cotta tile, tired shrubs and trees, and not an ounce of food in sight. The existing Spanish-style landscape was at odds with its traditional shingled home and with its owners, who love to entertain outdoors and to garden. Our plan was to welcome in a warmer, livelier environment with designated spaces to relax, welcome guests, and grow edible plants.

To make space for a potager, we reconfigured a rose garden that was past its prime. With excellent solar exposure and vertical fences for support, the vegetables nestled into willow-edged raised beds with ease. A potted herb garden, arranged atop an antique stone table, elevates the area from simply a spot to grow edibles to an intentional design element in the landscape.

Now, perennial edibles are woven into a series of experiential garden rooms that wrap around the house. This serves as a reminder that food can hold its own in a fairly formal garden setting. Overall, through the choices of materials and plantings, the landscape manages to balance several opposites all at once—old and new, formal and casual, practical and romantic, ornamental and edible, traditional and timeless.

The Garden Route

The side-yard access path has been reinvented as a pleasurable portal to the potager beyond. Dense hydrangea foliage creates a lush tunnel, with flowers used for cutting and salvias and geraniums to lure all manner of pollinators. The armillary sphere makes a fitting focal point at one end of the long gravel walkway.

Boxwoods and Blueberries

Structural planting is important at the front of the house, particularly the main entrance. In this case, we leaned heavily on the solid forms of boxwood hedges and globes, interspersed with drifts of compact blueberry bushes. Both species prefer the less-hot, east-facing location. Faux bois concrete furniture stands out from all the greenery and reinforces the whimsical woodland ambience.

← Make Your Bed

Formerly an underused concrete patio, this corner of the yard now has six low woven-willow raised beds that pack a lot of food production into relatively tight quarters, including perennial edibles—apples, clementines, Meyer lemons, and berries—lining the perimeter fence.

↑ Tasteful Tabletop

A never-ending supply of perennial herbs in terra-cotta pots sits on a stunning stone-and-wrought-iron workbench.

Secret Door

This magical gateway looks as though it leads to a garden wonderland, when in fact the only things it hides are the kitchen garden supplies and tools. It's exemplary proof that no part of a landscape, even utilities storage, is too mundane to be made beautiful.

La Vie en Rose

A profuse 'Cécile Brünner' archway leads from the backyard
to the blueberry courtyard in the front, enveloping passersby
in a heady wave of sweet perfume. The petals of this classic
French rambling rose can be added to salads, infused for teas,
or distilled into rose water and used in baking.

← Culinary Comforts

The ample outdoor kitchen is decked out with a wood-burning pizza oven and wreathed in wisteria, lavender, and potted kumquats. Garden produce—homegrown broccolini, lemons, tomatoes, basil, and more—inspires frequent pizza parties by the pool.

↑ Leading the Way

An eighteenth-century granite fountain brings purpose to the far edge of the backyard, drawing you in and hinting that there is more around the corner (specifically, the pathway to the kitchen garden).

Calm and Collected

Fruiting olives and culinary bay create a cohesive backdrop
to the garden, shifting focus to the fruit-laden kumquat tree.
A repeating scheme of flowering lavender, catmint, and
structured boxwood globes conveys an old-world elegance.

MULTIUSE SPACES

The more activities you can fit comfortably into the footprint of your outdoor areas, the more pleasure you will get from them. Careful planning is required, however, when you take a food forward approach, especially where space and sunlight are limited. To ensure generous elbow room for all parties, consider your intended functions for the yard before you begin, allowing enough room for gardening as well as other interests.

Instead of dividing the layout into separate zones (the standard practice in many outdoor settings), "stack" functions to allow multiple activities to take place within the same area. Try, for example, bench seating backed by tall planter beds, or gate arches that double as trellises. For the widest range of activities, design spacious courtyards or decks that can double as tracts for gathering and engaging. Even something as simple as a wide pathway can invite room for recreation— a game of catch, maybe, or archery.

The Details

Seating A variety of seating areas (and seating options within them) should ensure there is the right fit for any moment—a comfortable place to read or work, say, a small table for close conversations, a larger table for hosting, and a simple bench for admiring a view. Including such an assortment of seating may seem like overkill, but it will make an outdoor space feel more expansive and less stagnant over time.

Planting Strategy To keep any multitasking spaces in central areas looking spiffy, exercise restraint with plants. Consider varieties that are better behaved— such as leafy greens, root vegetables, and herbs—in high-traffic areas, for the easiest flow.

(Nothing kills the fun factor like a crowded pathway or overgrown planter.) Opt for dependability, and prevent frustration by avoiding incompatibility, like having fragile plants border the kids' play area or short-lived plants frame a central walkway.

Coordination Choose materials and any gear or equipment you may need so that they blend with each other rather than stand out. In an outdoor shower, for example, use the same hardware finishes (such as copper or silver) as in your light fixtures. When this isn't possible, add discreet storage pieces. Get creative with under-seat storage for cushions or exercise gear, or deck cabinets for storing games or spa towels.

When this site was converted from a lawn into a vegetable garden, the family of archers didn't want to give up their target practice space. By designing a straight central path and a small flagstone patio at the far end, both priorities are now in play.

WILD
WONDERLAND

AFTER DECADES SPENT DESIGNING GARDENS FOR OTHERS, an opportunity to design one for myself arose. On an acre (0.4 ha) of land high in the hills, this midcentury gem came on the market. The real draw was the land, which consisted mainly of concrete terraces, poison oak, and some thriving native oaks. The chance to breathe new life into this landscape was simply too good to pass up.

Travel memories informed my vision for the refuge the property might become. I was reminded of dwellings deep in the wilderness—overgrown areas with trodden grass paths and wildflowers springing up with abandon. A welcoming place that seems at once untouched and yet carefully tended, an ode to the symbiotic partnership between gardener and the natural world.

My goal was to create a base camp—part classroom, playground, and living environment—for future work, with license to experiment on a larger yet more personal scale. Our team could observe natural successes and failures of growing food in a wild setting, then develop new ideas and put them into practice.

Just a few years on, our central, low-water, native sedge meadow is now populated with regional flowers. The oaks serve as a rich habitat for great horned owls and acorn woodpeckers and the open, lower slope holds space for a diverse fruit orchard. Our go-to materials for construction come from reclaimed and regionally sourced lumber, stone, and metal. Each of these elements, along with the new and existing plantings, have their own story to tell and add meaning to the property's purposeful new lease on life.

Hilltop Harvests
More than 700 square feet (65 sq m) of terraced annual
food production sits just below the native meadow.

Flower Beacon

Interspersed throughout the *Carex pansa* (dune sedge) meadow are wildflowers— among them, native yarrow, poppies, penstemon, and erigeron—that serve as a landing strip for local pollinators.

← Water Wise

An outdoor shower is tucked conveniently around the corner, immersed in huckleberry and chain fern, with a native California grape happily smothering the shade arbor. No water goes to waste—the runoff feeds into a gray-water system that hydrates the orchard on the hillside below.

↑ Herb Steps

We're always looking for ways to blend hardscape and edibles. These natural timber steps were backfilled with soil rather than gravel, and planted with a collection of culinary herbs at either end. 'Elfin' thyme ground cover designates the walking path.

'Dragon's Tongue' →

These purple-striped beans are a favorite variety for their appearance, flavor, and name.

Gift Basket ↘

There's no shortage of 'Marnouar' and 'Hot Streak' tomatoes during the warm season. They make a perfect present for neighbors and guests.

Bountiful Berries ↓

Raspberries are among the most satisfying—and economical—berries to grow at home. They are vigorous in both root and limb, so plan accordingly with pruning, root containment, and trellising.

Tomato Tunnel → →

Repeating, plant-covered archways add a "secret garden" touch as well as a more practical, space-saving way to grow food all year long—tomatoes in summer and fall, and peas or sweet pea flowers throughout winter and spring.

Workshop Window

The dining structure was inspired by
an animal "blind," with narrow windows
such as those used to observe wildlife in
a clearing. The rustic lumber siding was
salvaged from a structure leveled in the
1906 San Francisco earthquake.

← A Step Above

The outdoor dining area, native meadow, and terraced vegetable garden function as a collective whole, intuitive to traverse and close to one another but not cluttered. In the meadow, two weathered steel planters filled with vegetables in clear view of the house allow me to easily keep track of the garden's health at a glance.

↑ Mission Control

Its ceiling hung with a rotating assortment of drying flowers and herbs, this potting bench is both a creative outlet and a utilitarian workstation (for more on this design, see page 212).

NATIVE EDIBLES

Undoubtedly, some of the best-performing plants in any landscape are those that also grow wild throughout your region (invasive species excluded). Native species have had centuries to adapt to the area's climate, soil, predatory animals, and insects, relying on natural selection to evolve into the most resilient, hardy versions of themselves—all traits that can work in our favor. Focusing on native plants, especially flowering species, is also the best way to give back to the wildlife all around. Over millennia, ecosystems evolve as animals and plants work in tandem. The more we can preserve this relationship, the better for flora *and* fauna.

Among the well-known West Coast native edibles are wild strawberry, huckleberry, yerba buena, and elderberry. Those in the southern United States may be more familiar with prickly pear or pawpaw, while those in the East are well acquainted with walnuts, currants, and mulberries. Often, versions of the same plant exist on multiple continents under different names—for example, uncultivated blueberries are called bilberry in England, huckleberry in parts of the US, and arándano in Chile. Most native berries and fruits are ideal candidates for turning into homemade preserves or syrups, and since they aren't readily available in grocery stores, it's a fun (and educational) exercise in expanding your palate. I encourage you to explore tasty plants indigenous to your own bioregion. Chances are, there's something familiar for you to get started with.

The Details

Sourcing Determining which natives to grow in your region and where to acquire them sometimes requires a bit of research. To get your hands on these little gems, you have three choices: Look for local plant nurseries that carry native edibles, propagate them from cuttings or rootstock, or start them from seed (this last option is best suited to flowers and smaller species).

Growing When choosing to include local edibles, consider the plant's growth habit. Some native species are untamable and thus not well suited to manicured landscapes. Others, such as ramps and mushrooms, aren't amenable to cultivation, and are best foraged in the wild, much as we may wish to grow our own.

Native *Vitis californica* grapes grow to roof height within a single season, produce prolific harvests each fall, and, afterward, put on a delightful display of red foliage to admire.

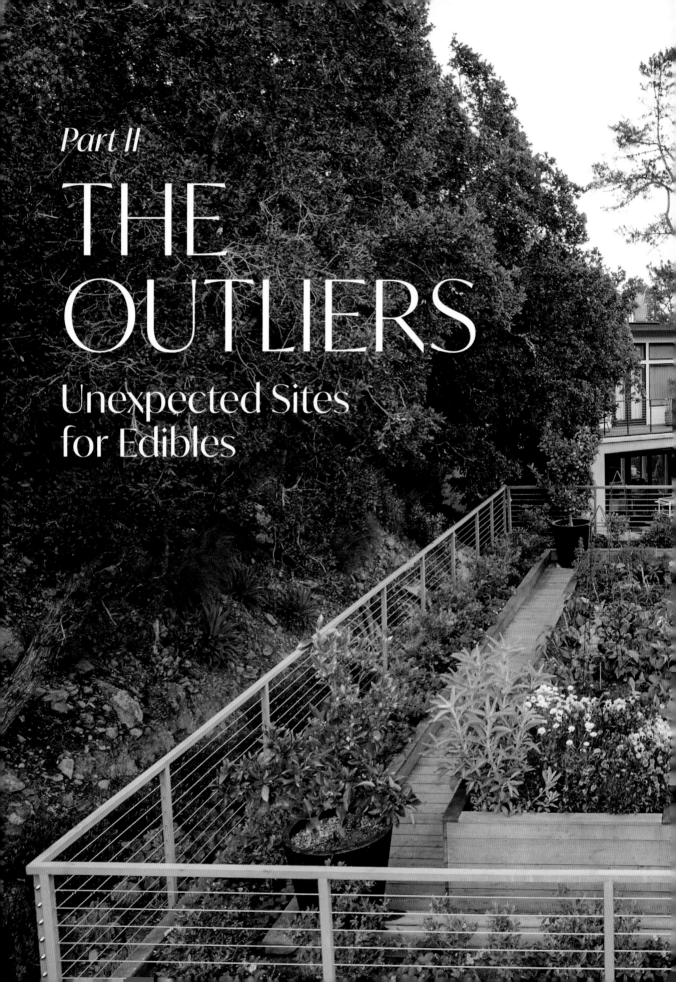

Part II

THE
OUTLIERS

Unexpected Sites
for Edibles

EVEN IF YOUR OUTDOOR SPACE LACKS ANY OBVIOUS
(read: flat and sunny) space for a traditional garden bed, don't
despair. There are many ways to bring edible plants to less-
expected, admittedly challenging sites. Here we explore how to
cultivate vegetables in raised beds in four wildly different areas:
meadows, woodlands, rooftops, and front yards. Each comes with
its own set of problems to solve, though the core principles of
growing food remain the same. The process for all four starts with
addressing available sunlight, and then locating the prime spots
for installing raised beds. (Creating a controlled environment is
especially important in these outliers.) You may have to work a bit
harder to meet their demands than you would in a more garden-
ready lot, but the fruits of your labor will certainly be as sweet.

THE EDIBLE MEADOW

Taking a light touch in the landscape doesn't mean that planting seasonal vegetables and other edibles is out of the question.

Growing vegetables and wildflowers within the same garden plan may seem like a contradiction: Wildflower meadows are inherently loose and carefree, while cultivating vegetables in beds generally calls for a more linear, well-tended approach. But juxtaposing one unrestrained, minimally manicured area with a more complex, densely planted bed has benefits for both. Here a kitchen garden spans the space between two lawns but still floats in the larger landscape, a fine example of working with empty space at large scale.

This sort of natural planting plan can be effective anywhere, really. Rather than looking unmoored, the raised beds appear as if carved out of the vivid pasture. The more open, meadowy areas extend the view, making the landscape feel larger. What's more, having a fair amount of negative space around cultivated beds gives the plants room to breathe, and the gardener more opportunity to admire them and to remember to put them to good use.

The garden, grill, and outdoor dining area feel nestled into the surrounding wildflower meadow while still remaining within clear sight of the house.

SECRETS TO SUCCESS

Create a Clearing

In a big expanse like a meadow, deciding where to situate a garden (or anything else) can feel daunting. As you scope out your own site, keep negative space and proportion in mind. The meadow aesthetic is most successful when the built elements are surrounded by open areas on all sides.

Carve Out Paths

Not all pathways need to be built in. Sometimes they can be formed from mowed strips, or slim trails planted with ground cover or lined with wood chips for a less-disruptive look. In this instance, we opted for minimal hardscape with trodden pathways that loosely mimic deer tracks.

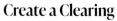

Establish Seating Areas

Arranging a seating area among the plants adds a purposeful feel to the garden-within-a-meadow arrangement, and it creates a destination as well. Here a large table and a grill combine to set the scene, bringing notice that this is as much a place for socializing and dining as it is for working the soil.

Accentuate with Wildflowers

To cultivate a wild, whimsical feel, surround your beds with flowers—such as poppies, coreopsis, Queen Anne's lace, nigella, cosmos, yarrow, and bachelor's buttons—that will keep reseeding to create an ever-evolving canvas of color. This method is perfect for meadows and cottage-inspired flower beds and will look best after the second year, when some species have self-sown and sprouted up irregularly. To enhance this natural look, take a more selective, less restrictive approach to weeding.

THE EDIBLE ROOFTOP

If you've run out of space on the ground to grow food, try looking up.

In general, I take a "leave no sunny space unplanted" approach to edible landscaping. Wherever there's a strong will to grow food, there's a way. Depending on a few logistical factors (most important: weight-bearing surfaces—more on this below), reclaiming rooftops for food production can make practical sense. Opportunities lie in flat, sun-drenched spots. For some, that may mean a rooftop, terrace, or balcony that can easily be converted to growing space, in beds or a collection of pots.

If you live in an area with deer or other predators, this is a very effective way to keep them from eating all your hard-won plants (birds can be an issue, of course, so seasonal coverings may be required). Be aware that such a high level of sun exposure means that during the hotter months, gardening is best done either first or last thing in the day. Keep in mind, too, that soil is heavy, so providing sufficient support for your rooftop garden is essential. Ask a structural engineer or architect if you are unsure your roof can handle the load. (If you live in a rental, consult with your landlord.) And to help reduce weight, use a lightweight soil mix with a high percolation rate.

This raised-bed garden was built atop a two-car garage roof. The surrounding edged beds are packed with (almost) more blueberries and strawberries than anyone could pick in peak season. Potted citrus trees thrive in each corner.

SECRETS TO SUCCESS

Establish Access

Make sure to allow easy entry to the garden, not only for yourself but for hauling all the tools and supplies you will need, including heavy bags of soil. (A ladder is not safe.) Here the rooftop has an exterior staircase. In other cases, access is granted via a second-story door that opens from inside the home. Depending on your site, there may be other ways to create safe exterior entries. Consult with a professional as needed.

Assess Drainage

Rooftop gardens require proper drainage. There are multiple ways to go about this. On this site, we allowed water to drain through gapped wood decking to a gutter on one side. Not only does it keep the space clean and ensure the plants aren't drowned, but it also reduces the weight on the structure.

Install Irrigation

You'll need water plumbed at the roof to hydrate your plants. It is much hotter, drier, and windier on exposed rooftops, and the lack of soil volume you would get by planting in ground or even in a large at-grade planter causes rooftop plants to dry out much more quickly than those down below. The solution is to "pulse" the irrigation by running it for much shorter durations, but more frequently.

Add Wind Protection

If the topography around your rooftop garden lacks trees or other natural wind breaks, consider building them in to protect overly exposed areas. This could include a screen, hedge, or high-sided planter. Mild wind can dry out the soil and dehydrate plant leaves; strong winds may cause branches to break and blossoms to blow away. (Occasionally, wind can create more severe damage.)

THE EDIBLE WOODLAND

Limited sunlight doesn't have to dim your chances of food in the forest.

The forest is certainly a niche location for growing food, but it's not without its rewards for any gardener who likes a challenge. Here the two main considerations are capturing available sunlight in summer (when the sun is higher) and protecting the plant beds from forest friends (aka predators). Even in summer, sunlight is sparse, so you'll have to seek out natural clearings or prune the tree canopy layer to improve light filtration. In wooded areas populated by deciduous trees, success can be higher for cool-season or early-spring crops—like brassicas (cabbages, broccoli, and such), some root vegetables, peas, and salad greens—when tree leaves are minimal or absent.

Sharing harvests with a host of hungry animals is another matter. The level of pest pressure in a forest garden depends on the location and circumstances. Some gardens can remain unprotected and unscathed for years, while others are almost immediately besieged. Beyond the many prevention avenues to explore (trapping, motion sensor lights and sounds, repugnant scents), the most reliable way to keep pests at bay is with a physical barrier. Building streamlined, lightweight wire covers for raised beds prevents animals from entering while preserving ease of access for humans. It maintains the natural beauty and splendor of the garden, too.

A terrace carved out of a thicket of redwoods creates additional space for cultivating annual food and flowers. The permanent protective screens make growing more vulnerable crops possible in this wildlife-rich, surprisingly sunny habitat.

SECRETS TO SUCCESS

Consider the Sunlight

Look for windows within the forest that receive more direct light than other areas, which can translate to more success with summer gardens. This may also call for trimming some of the canopy layer to improve growing conditions. Typically, growing a good winter garden, when the arc of the sun is lower, can be tricky.

Mind the Critters

In wooded areas where pest pressure can be intense, save your cage-protected and sunniest space for vegetables, then round out your garden plan with pest-resistant varieties of flowers (typically anything with natural oils and a strong odor; lavender and marigold, for instance, are off-putting to rabbits and deer). Here, the uncovered bed of the garden has been dedicated to a mix of annual and perennial herbs and blooms that even the rodents won't bother.

Design the Beds

Lower cages are convenient to work around and suitable for growing all but the tallest plants (and climbing varieties). The cages can be built square, but adding an angle to the top doors makes reaching into them from the lower side much easier (and adds an elegant design note). These have hinged doors and magnetic closures, but cages can also be built with sliding sides.

Keep Materials Minimal

There's already so much going on in the forest—visually and otherwise—that it's best to choose streamlined materials. Through the use of slim wooden framing and galvanized metal mesh, these walk-in cages remain unobtrusive. Maintaining lightweight, simple lines helps the structure blend in.

THE EDIBLE FRONT YARD

Take the often-underutilized front of the house from passive to purposeful without compromising on style.

Most front yards are limited to decorative lawns, which consume a lot of resources without any meaningful return on investment and are arguably among the least dynamic ornamental plantings. Yet, in many cases, front yards offer unparalleled sun exposure and hiding-in-plain-sight space.

Reimagining the possibilities by positioning food on the street makes a bold statement and drives up the curb appeal. It also invites visitors and neighbors to admire the view (and, with a little encouragement, to share in the bounty!). Maybe it will motivate them to reconsider their own front yard garden, too— my definition of a win-win.

Try positioning the vegetable beds alongside the walkway leading to the front door, where you will likely pass by multiple times a day and notice exactly when things are ready to harvest. The key to a successful food forward front yard is to be as thoughtful and deliberate with the elements that define your vegetable garden as you are with the design details of the house.

Each wing of this unique garden is packed full of annual vegetables and bright cutting flowers—a far cry from its former life as a lawn. Shorter plants, such as peppers, beans, and cabbage, fill the angled beds while taller varieties, namely fava beans, dahlias, and sunflowers, grow around the perimeter.

SECRETS TO SUCCESS

Avoid a Fortress Feel

I prefer front yard food unhampered by tall fences, but in areas with heavy deer traffic, like this one, the garden must be protected. Choose low-profile fencing that won't obstruct the view or the sunlight. Hog wire panels offer a modern farmhouse look; the larger squares help the fence appear more friendly and less formidable. As a bonus, the fencing can support vining edible plants.

Try a New Angle

The striking design of these planter beds is more than just an aesthetic choice. We thought outside of the expected (straight-sided, rectilinear) box and made use of unexpected angles to maximize space to grow food within the 25-by-35 foot (7.6 x 10.7 m) enclosure. All of the planting areas are within an easy arm's reach from the gravel pathways without having to stretch or bend over.

Mirror the Materials

The design elements (including paint color, surface materials, gate style, and even gravel color and type) were chosen to blend seamlessly with the existing architecture of the house and landscape. The charcoal lumber fencing matches the window trim of the house, creating a visual union between the two.

Make Yourself at Home

A small café table with a pair of chairs in the center of the bed draws the eye and invites relaxation in the space. It also serves as an impromptu harvest station. The owner of this east-facing garden drinks coffee and reads the paper each day as the sun comes up. At the same time, he is regularly observing when vegetables are at peak harvest and ready for the day's menu.

Part III

THE
BASICS

Edible Gardening Essentials

GARDENS ARE PART SCIENCE, PART ART. THOUGH those proportions certainly vary by location, you can't cultivate one successfully without embracing both. Aesthetic decisions about plants are interdependent on your hardiness zone, available sunlight, soil health, irrigation, and more. In the pages that follow, you'll find recommendations, techniques, and troubleshooting advice for those technical aspects of laying out your space for optimal growing conditions. From there, I'll share my favorite tools and accessories to help your days in the garden feel more efficient, organized, and most important, enjoyable.

Ready To HARVEST

- Kale
- Fava Beans
- Spinach
- Blueberries
- Strawberries
- Alpine Strawberries
- Lemons
- Yerba Buena
- Lettuce
- Herbs

Design Guide

My food forward approach to garden design centers on building an additional—namely, edible—layer into conventional, tried-and-true landscape principles. By viewing food through the same aesthetic lens as everything else in the landscape, you can create cohesive, substantive gardens that are as visually appealing as they are sustaining, and frankly, delicious.

The truth is, anybody can stick edible plants in a landscape. The real test is whether you will interact with, tend to, harvest, and enjoy them. Over many years of observing how thoughtful design sets our clients up for continued engagement with their gardens, we've landed on a few best practices that help ensure success.

The guidelines that follow provide insight into our design process. The concepts apply to in-ground, integrated plantings, mostly perennials. Knowing how to work with shapes, textures, colors, and other fundamental plant characteristics will help you compose a garden scheme that feels considered, original, and personal to you—and that will encourage you to grow more food, with confidence and care, wherever you live.

Layout

One of the most fundamental steps in designing a landscape is determining where the key elements will go, as well as how they will share the available space and flow together. My approach differs slightly from the norm because it encourages you to consider where and how food will be incorporated into the layout from the very beginning, not as an afterthought.

First, we must consult our beloved patron, the sun. Assessing and mapping sun exposure and its travel patterns across your yard will serve as a launchpad for all the great ideas to follow (more on this on page 174). The next step is making a list of all your desired elements—dining terraces, pathways, pools, firepits, outdoor kitchens, orchards, kitchen gardens, and the like. Then it's time to determine what goes where, based on your observations of how the sun moves through each area of your yard and on your design priorities. When dividing up the space, it's important to consider proportion and movement: how every element relates to the others in size, and how you will access each space. Wider pathways should flow through the primary areas, while narrow secondary paths or stepping stones can connect peripheral zones.

As you create your layout, continue to challenge the convention of placing food away from the main "living spaces" and think creatively about how to do the opposite. This is where the design process gets fun! Take a moment to imagine:

• An outdoor dining area framed by stone raised beds for berries and herbs that double as seat walls during larger gatherings

• A kitchen garden in the soil above a retaining wall that holds back the slope next to the house

• A fence that screens the neighboring property supporting espaliered pears or cherries

• A planter next to the outdoor kitchen filled with easy-to-reach culinary herbs

Remember, even small additions can go a long way toward creating a more interactive and interesting space.

This deck with a cedar spa tub surrounded by raised beds proves that relaxation and food production can happily coexist in close quarters. On the upper slopes, berries and fruit trees supply seasonal additions to morning smoothies.

Tending

Deciding what to plant, and how much of it, involves a number of visual and practical considerations. One factor that's often overlooked is the amount of time and energy you're willing and able to commit to the garden. Create a planting plan that fits your schedule by choosing appropriate species and quantities of edibles, whether that's vegetables that need frequent attention or fruit trees that are more hands-off.

One metaphor that has helped me is to liken growing edibles to raising children. Annual vegetables need watchful care and attention, much like toddlers. Keeping them well fed and secure as they get established is the top priority. They need to be tended to in short and frequent bursts, but there's joy to be had in watching their rapid and exuberant growth. Herbs and berries are the tweens of the edible landscape: Not *quite* self-sufficient, they are still tender enough to rely on semi-regular maintenance and supervision. Fruit trees, much like young adults, are generally low maintenance, with only the occasional check-ins. What they give back is a distinct character that has developed largely (but not entirely) on its own. As with most relationships, it's a two-sided affair.

See below for a closer look at the routine care and maintenance needs for each category of edibles. Ensuring from the start that you can put in the appropriate amount of time and energy for the plants you've chosen will affect the health and long-term benefits of all.

Plant Type	Care and Maintenance Schedule
Vegetables	Weekly visits at minimum to check on their health and well-being, increasing to 1 to 3 times per week during peak harvest seasons. Feed every 1 to 3 months.
Herbs and Berries	Herbs are ideally visited as needed to harvest; berries should be visited almost daily when in season (which lasts anywhere from 1 to 4 months, depending on the type). Feed 1 to 3 times a year, with one good pruning.
Fruit Trees	Visits as needed during harvest season. Most deciduous trees require harvesting for a 1- to 2-month period (citrus can be ongoing). Feed 1 or 2 times a year; prune once a year.

Your Plant "Palette"

Choosing plants for any new project involves compiling a long list and then whittling that down to a shorter final selection. This is the time to imagine growing the foods you most enjoy eating! Start dreaming of edible species you would love to harvest for your favorite recipes. Of course, you'll also want to consider ornamentals and pollinator plants.

The general direction of plant choices will be influenced by your climate (see page 176 for more on this) and individual style preferences. For example, you might lean toward cottage gardens, which flaunt flowers in an abundance of colors and textures. In that case, you'll end up with a longer list than someone who favors traditional or modern gardens that emphasize repetition and a limited color palette, like a scheme of mainly blueberries, grasses, and lavender, for example.

The process of narrowing down all the possible options involves researching plant varieties to ensure they are suited to the site, factoring in climate, water needs, care requirements, and so on. Make sure, too, that the scale and behavior of the plants are the right fit for the space. Situating a large, unwieldy artichoke next to a narrow path, for example, or a rambling thorny blackberry next to the children's trampoline, may not be the most practical. You want to avoid anything that might become a nuisance, however eye-catching it may be.

The goal is to end up with a list of plants that contains enough diversity without becoming a jumble of colors and textures. Often, a more refined palette (meaning a shorter list) makes it easier to create a cohesive landscape. It's tempting to get excited about adding lots of variety, but in the end, streamlining your selection almost always results in a garden that's more appealing and easier to tend.

Page 166 offers a few key design considerations to keep in mind as you develop a plant palette of your own.

Drifts of *Salvia nemorosa* and 'Provence' lavender stand out among a sea of green *Sesleria autumnalis* (autumn moor grass) and the more formal 'Green Spire' euonymus and clipped pittosporum globes. Small olive, satsuma, avocado, and pineapple guava trees complete the Mediterranean-inspired palette.

SHAPE

Plants grow in a boundless array of shapes, which are defined in landscape terms as globes, vases (or fountains), columns, umbrellas, and on and on. Composing a landscape with a variety of plant shapes will create rhythm and contrast, but don't get too hung up on all these different qualifiers. Ultimately, the most important balance to strike is that between what we call "hard" and "soft" plants.

"Hard" foundation plants provide a grounding element in your landscape design. These are like the walls of a house, offering structure and substance and a base for the "soft," more informal or flamboyant plants in your beds. This juxtaposition between more rigid (hard) and organic (soft) shapes is crucial to creating a dynamic landscape.

"Hard" edibles include:
Artichoke, bay laurel, compact blueberry bushes, dwarf citrus trees, guava and pineapple guava, olive, rosemary topiary

"Soft" edibles include:
Alpine strawberry, anise hyssop, currants, geranium, grapes and other vines, huckleberry, lavender, lemon verbena

TEXTURE

Landscapes are more compelling when they include a variety of contrasting and complementing textures. I like to expand the definition of texture to include overall leaf shape as well. We can all picture the difference between a wispy garden grass and a bold banana leaf, and we know what it feels like when a plant's surface edges are rough, smooth, or serrated. Strappy or spiky leaves (such as iris or agave) contrast beautifully with the dense, small leaves of olive or pomegranate trees, just as the ruffled foliage of heuchera or alpine strawberry pairs with the smooth texture of ginger or fatsia.

Edibles with incredible texture:
Artichoke, asparagus, banana, chives, fig, ginger, lemongrass, mulberry, rhubarb, sage, sorrel

COLOR

In the landscape, color refers to a plant's foliage as well as seasonal flowers and fruit. Just as you would design a room with a unifying color palette in mind (considering the relationship between the wall color, artwork, and furnishings), take the overall color scheme of your landscape into consideration. Perhaps you want to evoke a certain mood—cool colors (blue, white, purple) suggest relaxation and calm, whereas warm colors (yellow, orange, red) are energetic and bold. Aside from cool and warm, you can take this concept a step further and focus on tonality, for example, exploring combinations of rich jewel tones or soft pastels. You may wish to embrace a monochromatic palette, committing to one accent color in multiple shades, such as light violets to mid-purple lavenders to dark purple salvias. Or make a statement with contrasting colors, such as purple and yellow or blue and orange.

Edibles for pops of color:
Chartreuse oregano, chives, citrus, lavender, persimmon, pink chintz thyme, purple Anjou pear, purple basil, purple kale, pomegranate, stone fruit blossoms, strawberries

Composition

Below are four principal functions plants can serve in the composition of your landscape. Each plant has its own characteristics; many can fill more than one role, depending on location and other factors. For example, a citrus tree is often included as a specimen plant on its own, but when grouped with other citrus trees in a hedge, it becomes a background filler. Certain plants may be more suited to one use than another, such as bright flowers for accents and grasses arranged in drifts, but generally, it's how you use a plant in the overall garden composition that determines its function.

Specimen A single plant that holds its own as a focal point in the landscape because of its color, shape, or strong silhouette. Persimmon and mulberry trees are examples (among others) of specimen plants I like in a landscape.

Accent A plant or cluster of plants used sparingly, to draw the eye through the landscape and create a statement or punctuation. By design, accent plants stand out from the rest—picture the bold silver-gray foliage of an artichoke against a mass of dark green grasses, or strawberries dotted along a pathway.

Filler A plant with more uniform, less showy foliage that acts as a backdrop to accent or specimen plants. These are often planted in groups or serve as hedges. Currants, bay laurel, and pineapple guava make excellent edible fillers.

Drift One species of plant that is grouped en masse to create a shape that flows through the landscape like water wending around a boulder. A drift can be composed of any plant type, and multiple drifts might weave or blend together at the edges. A few favorites for this planting approach include sages, lemongrass, and strawberries.

Drifts of *Sesleria* 'Greenlee' (moor grass) and *'Festuca mairei'* (Atlas fescue) spill down this hillside, merging with colorful accents of 'Hidcote' lavender and *Teucrium chamaedrys* (wall germander) plus a few textural fillers: 'Green Spire' Euonymus, creeping rosemary, and 'Little Rev' flax lily.

Layering

Natural landscapes are made up of layers of plants that together weave a rich tapestry, and there are ample opportunities for growing edibles in every layer. The overstory is the highest layer of foliage (typically, a tree canopy), which can cast shade on anything below. The height and density of the overstory can have a significant impact on the lower plant layers and the proportions of the landscape as a whole. Next comes the understory (or mid-layer), which is made up of medium-size plants, including smaller trees and shrubs, that grow below the tree canopy. Then there is the ground cover: the layer of plant life close to the soil surface. These low-growing, spreading plants are helpful for erosion control and weed suppression.

Mimicking these layers by varying heights and shapes will make your own designs feel more natural, giving an organic sense of depth within a planting bed. Generally, trees and tall plants are used to provide scale, create focal points, frame the space, or divide it into smaller sections, alternatively making an area feel more wide and expansive or secluded and cozy. Along with vines, trees can be especially helpful in hiding fences or other boundaries and supplying shade. Shrubs and other medium-size plants fill in the space between the ground and the tree canopy. And there are often layers within this mid-layer: small shrubs, flowers, and grasses of different shapes and sizes. At the ground level, small grasses and creeping plants cover the soil and offer open space above. By the same token, layers can also be used strategically to create bold landscapes with crisp lines that defy natural rules. Below is a chart of edible plants to consider adding into the layers of your own garden; turn to the Plant Index beginning on page 241 for more options.

Layer	Edibles to Consider
Overstory	Trees such as apple, citrus, fig, mulberry, peach, pear, plum, walnut
Understory	Shrubs such as blueberry, Chilean guava, currants, gooseberry, huckleberry, rosemary; and vines like blackberry, grape, hops, kiwifruit, passion fruit
Ground Cover	Creeping plants such as chamomile, oregano, strawberry, thyme, yerba buena; and roots such as ginger, sunchokes, turmeric

Low *Carex divulsa* grasses frame the pathway, with mixed layers of increasingly larger shrubs and trees (including ferns, rhododendrons, oakleaf hydrangea, sycamore, and oaks), screening the fence and providing a sense of scale with the house.

Gardening Guide

Gardening is nothing if not nuanced, and there are different traditions, methods, and practices for plant cultivation all over the world. The greatest teacher is trial and error. Your second-best teacher? An experienced gardener. That's why I started the Backyard Farm Company, to support our clients in maintaining their edible landscapes after planting. The mission extends beyond simple upkeep, to include detailed gardening education and mentoring so that gardeners at all experience levels can understand the ins and outs of growing their own food in any space or season.

What follows is a crash course that offers much of the same education. Use this information to help set up or streamline your raised beds, where the majority of vegetable production will take place. All of the recommendations and guidelines that follow are designed to help you get to know the conditions within your own garden, build confidence, and set you on the path to success as you learn to grow your own food.

Sunlight

Sunlight is the single most important factor when it comes to assessing the potential for growing food. Naturally, then, one of the first steps in planning your outdoor space will be to determine what part(s) of your landscape receive the most sun.

Thanks to technology, it's quite easy to properly evaluate the sunlight in any garden. I rely on an app called Sun Seeker, which takes out the guesswork and shows the path of the sun throughout the entire year. Within minutes, the app allows me to gauge the sunlight hours in every corner of a property. You can accurately pinpoint specific areas of your space to determine where and what to grow.

There are, of course, time-honored, pre-smartphone ways to assess sunlight in your garden, like drawing an old-fashioned "sun map." Start by sketching a simple, bird's-eye view of your landscape: On a clear day, go out to your yard at eight a.m., noon, and four p.m., and each time pencil in the areas that are covered in shade. By the end of the day, the lightest areas on your page will reflect the areas with the least amount of shade. The arc of the sun changes throughout the year, so you'll need to complete this exercise again in each season to get a full picture of the growing conditions. Take note of existing trees, fences, and buildings that may cast shade on different areas. Trees cast more shade when they have all their leaves in summer, but fences and buildings are often an obstacle in winter, when the angle of the sun is lower.

MORE SUNLIGHT = MORE PRODUCE

The chart below describes the edible plant possibilities based on the number of minimum hours of available sunlight required for each per day. Keep in mind that not all periods of sun throughout the day are created equal. Therefore, it's important to consider not only the quantity of sunlight but also the quality, which is basically the time of day. Morning light, which is less intense, is preferred by plants that don't love the heat. Afternoon sun is great for ripening summer fruits but can scorch and stress more-sensitive crops.

Available Sunlight	Edibles to Consider
Greater than 8 hours	Fruit trees and fruiting crops including tomatoes, peppers, squash, cucumbers, melons, and eggplants, which thrive with as much sun as possible—a full 12 hours, if they can get it!
6 to 8 hours	Full-sun crops such as blueberries, brassicas, beans, and root vegetables. At this rate of sunlight, some tomatoes and other crops in the above category can still grow well; for best results, stick to smaller varieties (like cherry tomatoes), and keep in mind that you may see slower growth and reduced production.
4 to 6 hours	Leafy greens (particularly lettuces), radishes, turnips, bok choy, and a few herbs. Small, faster-growing crops will have the best chance at success. You can also try understory berries such as alpine strawberries and huckleberries.
Fewer than 4 hours	This amount of sunlight is insufficient for growing meaningful quantities of food. Without enough sunlight, plants grow very slowly and are more susceptible to pests and disease in their weakened state.

ORIENTATION

In general, if you live in the Northern Hemisphere, you want to have as much southern exposure as possible for your garden; the opposite holds true for those in the Southern Hemisphere (in other words, aim for northern exposure). This orientation should ensure maximal sunlight throughout the year, even with the lower angle of the sun in winter.

For raised beds, it's generally best to orient planter boxes east to west. Bear in mind that this is subjective and can depend on distinct conditions of your garden site and its existing topography. Nevertheless, with the longer edges of the bed pointing east to west, you can plant taller crops on the northern side so the shade falls on the pathway instead of other crops. I tend to think of the north side as the "back" of the garden, since that is where the majority of shade will accumulate.

Climate

Many countries map individual growing zones (commonly known as hardiness zones), which are determined by the average minimum temperature for each region. It's easy to find your zone online (in the US, visit the USDA website for an interactive map). Knowing your growing zone allows you to identify which plants will thrive in your area, since zones are often listed directly on the plant label and in catalog descriptions (and in the Plant Index beginning on page 241).

Because this method of categorization relies solely on minimum temperatures, however, it has limitations. What the zones do not account for are microclimates, which exist in places where the local weather conditions, including wind, air temperatures, humidity, and solar radiation, are markedly different from surrounding areas. These variables result from a few different factors, like the topography (and its effect on available light, for example) and proximity to large bodies of water (which can create conditions like coastal fog). The best way to think of microclimates is as if you're zooming in on the minutiae of weather patterns in one valley, which may differ from the next valley over. You can find resources online to determine your own microclimate.

Cold zones are locations that experience cold temperatures and a short warm season, and are cataloged by lower numbers on the hardiness scale (for example, USDA Zones 1 to 7). In these areas, perennial plants will need to be frost-hardy to survive winter outdoors, and any cold-sensitive plants such as citrus or avocado will need to be brought inside or protected with a frost blanket. You may have to pause vegetable production for the winter (especially where the ground freezes or stays buried in snow) or grow these plants in a greenhouse.

Warm zones experience warmer temperatures and a shorter or nonexistent cool season. Much of the southern US seaboard (closer to the equator) is categorized as USDA Zones 8 to 13 and rarely experiences frost or freezing temperatures. Subsequently, more plants can grow year-round in these locations.

Warmer is not necessarily always better, however. In fact, some plants, most notably deciduous fruit trees and berries, require a minimum number of "chill hours" (anywhere from 100 to 1,000 hours below 45°F/7°C) during dormancy to produce fruit. In warmer climates, it's best to choose varieties with low chill hour requirements. You can find this information by searching online for your specific region.

Growing Seasons

Generally speaking, as winter wanes and warmer temperatures and longer days signal the start of spring, seeds germinate and plants come out of dormancy. Each plant variety has its own schedule of growth, however. To ensure that your landscape is lively year-round, consider the seasonal attributes of each plant, and aim to include varieties that bloom and fruit at different times.

For the purposes of food production in most locations, we can simplify the year into two main categories: a cool season and a warm season, with spring and fall as transition periods (or more poetically, the shoulder seasons) between these two parts of the year. Turn the page for a brief look at the produce best suited for each growing season.

BOLTING EXPLAINED

Bolting (as shown in the photo at left) occurs when cool-season crops switch all of their energy toward producing flowers and seeds, which happens at the end of their life cycle. This change is often based on rising temperatures or other natural occurrences. When you see a brassica like kale start to develop a tall stem and flower, that's a signal that it's time to harvest the whole plant and plant something else in its place. By the time you notice lettuce, arugula, or radishes bolting, they may already be too bitter, spicy, or tough to enjoy. Alternatively, you can leave flowering plants for the bees to enjoy and for collecting seeds to plant next season.

Most warm-season plants reproduce through the seeds inside their fruit and, therefore, don't tend to bolt like cool-season crops. A pepper plant, for example, produces seeds inside every pepper, so when nature starts to signal that conditions are getting too cold or dark, the plant simply starts to slow down and die, having already done its job, theoretically, of reproducing.

COOL SEASON

Cool-season crops prefer air temperatures below 75°F (24°C) and can withstand light frost. These plants will produce more (and taste better!) when grown in cool weather, which means it's usually best to plant them in spring and fall. Growing them in hotter temperatures will likely result in stunted growth or bolting (see page 177)—in other words, little to no usable harvest.

If, however, you live in an area with mild summers, you may be able to grow these throughout the warmer months. You may also be able to extend your growing season by planting cool-season crops in the shadier areas of your garden during warmer months, where they are less likely to overheat. (This is also convenient, since most of the warm-season crops wouldn't grow as well in that shadier spot anyway, so it's a win-win form of crop planning.)

When planning for the cool season, think of the hearty greens you'd enjoy adding to soups and stews, and starchy root vegetables you're likely to roast. Amazingly, brassicas, root crops, and alliums can become sweeter after a frost, due to plants converting their starch stores into sugars to protect themselves from the cold. At right, a few of my cool-season picks:

Alliums Garlic, leeks, onions, shallots (onions can be grown year-round; there are "long day," "short day," and "day neutral" varieties for different seasons)

Brassicas Bok choy, broccoli, cabbage, cauliflower, collard greens, kale, kohlrabi

Greens Arugula, chard, chicories, lettuce, mizuna, radicchio, spinach

Herbs Cilantro, dill, parsley

Legumes Fava beans, peas

Roots Beets, carrots, parsnips, radishes, turnips

WARM SEASON

Warm-season crops grow best when air temperatures reach 75 to 95°F (24 to 35°C). Many of these crops should be planted in spring and will not be ready to harvest until peak summer, but they can keep producing into late summer or early fall. They cannot survive frost unprotected.

During this season, gardeners typically grow plants that produce fruit, rather than eating the leaves or roots (as always, there are exceptions to this rule). Because the process of producing fruit is more energy intensive than growing greenery or roots, warm-season crops such as eggplants and pumpkins require additional fertilizing and are often referred to as "heavy feeders." (A few cool-season crops are considered heavy feeders, too, namely garlic and large brassicas.) Warm-season plants (and warmer regions as a whole) are often plagued by more pests and diseases than cold-weather ones, as there is no frost to kill off the harmful insects or slow the spread of bacteria, fungus, and viruses. (For more on managing pests and diseases, see page 187.)

Though they can be a bit more high-maintenance than their cool-weather counterparts, warm-season crops benefit from the increased sunlight driving the production of sugars, with exceptional results. Think sweet, juicy, and colorful crops in vibrant reds, oranges, and yellows. At right, a few of my warm-season favorites:

Cucurbits Cucumbers, gourds, melons, pumpkins, squash

Grains Amaranth, corn, quinoa, wheat

Herbs Basil, tarragon

Legumes Bush beans, pole beans

Nightshades Eggplants, peppers, potatoes, tomatillo, tomatoes

Healthy Soil

Whenever I'm asked why our gardens look consistently full and abundant, the answer is simple: It starts with the soil. After sunlight, soil health has the most impact on any plant's potential, and in the case of edible varieties, on its flavor, too. The healthier the soil, the more robust and nutrient-dense the crops. This is the main reason homegrown produce tastes superior to anything store bought.

Most people don't realize that soil is a living organism and needs to be treated as such. When it's healthy, soil is a wonderful, complex melting pot of diverse biota. Beneficial microorganisms forge symbiotic relationships with plants to support their survival, processing and trading nutrients for sugars. Our primary role as gardeners is to ensure favorable conditions for those transactions to take place.

Following are six tips for fostering healthy soil in a vegetable garden, specifically in raised beds. Keep these guidelines in mind as you're starting out and in subsequent seasons, as you no doubt continue to build on your early gains.

1. Know What You're Aiming For

Soil is the foundation of every healthy garden (quite literally). Once you understand the fundamentals of soil composition, you are on your way to a successful harvest. Optimal soil for growing vegetables looks rich and loamy; you should see worms and smaller bugs, and a mix of fine and larger crumbs the color of 70 percent cacao chocolate. It has a sweet, earthy smell. Healthy soil boosts any plant's immunity from pests and disease and helps it stay hydrated longer, meaning you have to water less.

2. Get It Tested

It's rare to start gardening with naturally optimal soil. Without a soil test, you'll have to rely on trial and error to figure out what adjustments your plants need to thrive. (Throwing in some compost before planting is usually a good guess, but that's often not enough to make up for nutrient deficiencies and imbalances.) Start with having your soil tested by an agricultural lab or university cooperative extension, which will provide the precise information needed to create the perfect growing medium. You may discover you need to adjust your soil's pH (see box, page 183) level or that it requires a supplement like nitrogen (the most commonly recommended amendment). I suggest testing annually to monitor the results of your amendments, until the levels are relatively stable and you have a better understanding of how to keep them consistent.

3. Start Strong

Whether you're growing food in raised beds or containers, or directly in the ground, try to get your hands on the best soil you can find. For planters, new soil is necessary; in the ground, you'll want to supplement with compost. In most cases, that means buying a local soil mix from a landscape material supplier that can be delivered in bulk by the cubic yard or meter. (This is also more convenient, and more affordable, than buying soil in bags.) Look for a blend that consists of native soil, some compost or manure for nutrients, and, finally, materials conducive to drainage, such as lava rock, sand, or composted wood chips, all of which contribute to good texture.

4. Feed the Soil, Not the Plants

If I can impart one crucial piece of advice when it comes to growing your own food, it is to keep the soil microbiology healthy and thriving. Add compost and other organic additives to ensure macro- and micronutrients, the critical building blocks of plant life, are readily available.

For annual vegetable gardens, at minimum, add a high-quality organic compost in spring and fall, just before planting new crops. Compost has multiple long-term benefits, including adding more microorganisms and improving the soil's texture and moisture retention. Other amendments you may need to add periodically depend on the results of your soil test (see step 2). Worm castings, coconut coir, or biochar can further benefit the texture and biodiversity of soil.

5. Replenish Regularly

For raised beds, in addition to fertilizing before planting in spring and fall, you'll want to add feedings in the months in between. The initial supply of nitrogen should last around three months (the same goes for potting soil sold in bags), so I recommend adding a sprinkle of all-purpose fertilizer at the midway point of the seasons. For flowering crops, you can try a sprinkle of bloom-food fertilizer, which has a slightly lower nitrogen ratio than all-purpose.

In-ground perennials need regular care and feeding, too. Larger, longer-lived plants require greater quantities of fertilizer, but less frequently. A generous spring feeding is generally sufficient to satisfy them through the year. Feed fruit trees and berries in early spring, as they wake up from dormancy, by adding a 1-inch-thick (2.5 cm) layer of aged manure or rich compost around their root zone. (Take care that the material does not touch the trunk, which can cause rot or fertilizer burn.) For best results, top this layer with wood chip mulch to retain moisture. If perennial plants are young or struggling, fertilize and mulch again at the end of spring. Alternatively, you can use a premixed fruit fertilizer. Some fruits, like blueberries, need additional acid fertilizer (often labeled for rhododendrons and azaleas) to lower the soil's pH. No matter which fertilizers you are using, make sure to follow the instructions on the packaging. Excessive fertilizing can reduce harvests, attract aphids, and even kill plants, so aim to get it just right without going overboard.

6. Keep Up the TLC

With regular care, your soil will improve over time. Remember: Soil is a living thing, and as such, needs air (porosity), water (hydration), and the cycling of organic matter and nutrients (food) to thrive. Try to keep the soil from drying out completely, getting waterlogged, or becoming too compact, which affects the survival of vital microorganisms; the best way to accomplish this is by irrigating it regularly (see page 185), adding drainage, and amending with compost. Even if you aren't growing vegetables in a particular bed or season, you need to keep tending to the soil regularly. Ongoing care should keep you from having to start from scratch the following season.

THE pH BALANCE OF SOIL

Vegetables generally grow best in soil with a moderate pH level, around 6.5, so aim for something within the range of 6.3 to 6.8. To raise the pH of your soil, amend it with agricultural lime. Conversely, if you need to lower the soil's pH, add elemental sulfur. (Once you've sent your soil to the lab for analysis, as discussed on page 181, you should have a more precise idea of what amendments to add and how much of each.) It can take months for these amendments to adjust the pH range, though, so be patient before testing again or adding more.

Irrigation

Without question, you need a water source near your garden. At the very least, a regular hose for easy hand watering, after planting, and on a regular basis afterward. Keep in mind that when you start with healthy soil full of thriving microbes and organic matter, water will be retained in greater measure, making your job that much easier.

In drier climates that need seasonal irrigation, I strongly recommend installing a drip system, with lines that irrigate roots directly. This will save water (less evaporation, and fewer weeds, too), and since water doesn't collect on the leaves or splash soil onto the plants, there is less chance of spreading fungal and bacterial diseases, resulting in healthier plants. An automatic irrigation timer provides a consistent watering schedule (which reduces plant stress) and makes daily watering one less thing to worry about (reducing human stress)! Even with automatic irrigation, however, you'll need to keep an eye on your plants and check the moisture level of the soil regularly.

A note of caution: Very dry soil can become hydrophobic, meaning it looks wet on the top but is actually completely dry underneath and won't absorb water. That's why it's always important to check moisture at the root zone a few inches (6 to 8 cm) deep. To remedy, mix the soil and soak until hydrated.

How much water your garden will need depends on the properties of your soil, the size of your beds, and your microclimate (as noted on page 176). Also take into account *what* you're watering. Trees and other large perennial plants with established root systems prefer less-frequent, longer durations of watering (thirty minutes three times per week is a good benchmark). Smaller (or younger) plants with shallow root systems, particularly annual vegetables, thrive when watered in frequent short intervals (think ten minutes every day). Remember that seedlings need more frequent waterings than mature plants, which can get by with less. Insufficient watering and overwatering are both detrimental to plants and can drastically affect your harvests, so aim for consistency.

Drip tubing with emitter holes every 6 inches (15 cm) delivers a slow and steady supply of water directly to the root zone, keeping the soil evenly moist.

Troubleshooting

If your plants aren't looking quite right, keep the following in mind as you try to diagnose possible causes:

1. Environment

First, rule out any significant temperature fluctuations, which in extreme cases may cause frost or sunburn. Other environmental conditions such as wind, severe rain, or hail can cause visible damage to leaves. Remember, plants not adapted to your climate or the current season may struggle.

2. Pests and Disease

Check for common signs of pests—for example, holes or edges of foliage that have been nibbled away, or deposits of "frass" (insect poop). Always check the undersides of leaves, where tiny insects can hide or lay their eggs. Disease (whether bacterial, viral, or fungal) can also affect plants. Familiarize yourself with the symptoms of the most prevalent, such as powdery mildew and leaf spot. Check your local university extension program for expert help identifying pests and disease.

3. Water

Monitor the soil moisture a couple inches (5 cm) deep and make sure it is damp but not soggy. If leaves are turning brown, it could mean plants are not being watered consistently. Yellowing leaves may mean too much water or poor drainage.

4. Nutrients

If no pests are found and the soil moisture level is consistent, the culprit is likely a nutrient imbalance. Over- and under-fertilizing both have consequences and should be remedied. Of the two, under-fertilizing is by far the most common problem. It's easy to forget that plants need extra feeding throughout the growing season. Keep an eye out for the telltale signs of nutrient deficiency: slow growth or small, stunted plants; pale yellow foliage; dull leaves; bolting while the plant is still immature, before it has fruited or produced a leafy crop. Sometimes the best fix is a dose of all-purpose fertilizer mixed into the soil surface. This broad-spectrum feed covers all the primary essential plant nutrients and minerals. A multivitamin for plants, if you will. (You *can* overfeed your plants with fertilizer, however. For best results, always consult the instructions on the packaging.)

PROTECTION FROM PESTS GREAT AND SMALL

The best way to prevent frustrating insects and critters from creating problems is to plan ahead. First, if you live in an area with deer, be sure that your garden is completely protected with fencing. If you don't have an existing fenced-in area on your property, you may need to set up tall (6-foot/1.8 m) fencing around your garden. Beyond this first line of defense, here are a few more categories of physical barriers to consider.

Bird Netting With 1-inch (2.5 cm) holes, this netting won't keep anything smaller or more tenacious than a bird out of the garden, but it has the benefit of being nearly invisible from a distance. To prop the netting up above the plants, create support hoops out of sections of 9-gauge wire with the two ends secured in the ground. Use irrigation staples (large U-shaped metal fasteners, also used for drip irrigation lines, which you insert by hand) to attach the netting securely to the ground on all sides.

Insect Netting There are two types of cover cloths: insect (essentially mosquito) netting and thicker woven cloths (known in the landscape trade as insulating row covers), which keep out insects but also create a slight greenhouse effect, making them more practical in cooler climates. These coverings can be installed in the same fashion as bird netting.

Cloches A cloche (from the French, for "bell") is essentially a miniature cover used to shield particularly at-risk plants (such as lettuce or cabbage) from critters. Cloches can be made of wire mesh (as shown at right), wicker, or glass; each material serves a practical purpose and offers its own opportunity for garden decor.

Gopher Wire To protect raised beds and containers from gophers, work from the ground up. Attach ½-inch (1.3 cm) wire mesh (also known as hardware cloth or gopher wire) at the bottom of the bed, securing it to the wood base with staples. If aboveground critters like raccoons or squirrels are an issue, consider building permanent enclosures for your garden beds out of the same wire: You'll need to construct a wooden frame above the beds, with hinged doors or easily removable sections for harvesting (for an example of this type of wooden frame, see page 144).

Crop Planning

A crop plan is a layout of an edible garden (either a simple sketch or detailed diagram) that helps determine what plants go where for each growing season. You can rely on it to choose the ideal location for each crop type, create a more targeted (less costly) shopping list (or seed-starting list), and stay on top of succession planting for consistently timed harvests. Crop plans are also a useful reference for plant rotation, allowing you to repeat past successes and avoid future failures.

To create your crop plan, you'll need to consider multiple factors: Environmental conditions such as your climate and season will play a huge role in what you can plant and when. Your chosen plants' sun and space requirements, height (and whether or not it requires a support structure), and crop type (single or multiple harvest) are equally important. And last but not least, take into account your harvest goals (based on your household size, how frequently you like to cook, and so on); you may want to consider succession planting (planting multiple rounds of the same crop).

BEST PRACTICES

• Plant faster-growing crops near the front or entrance of the garden, where it's easier to keep an eye on them and harvest as needed. Place long-term or single-harvest crops (like onions, garlic, or winter squash) in the farther beds, since they don't need constant attention.

• Some tender plants, such as lettuce, may benefit from afternoon shade. As a rule, however, take care to ensure that taller, larger crops will not block sunlight.

• Group plant families together. Brassicas like broccoli and kale will thrive in the same bed; nightshades such as eggplants and peppers happily grow side by side.

• Plant herbs or flowers, such as calendula and marigold, at the corners or edges of beds, to add pops of color and attract pollinators.

• Leave empty space for replanting successions of quick crops (such as radishes and butterhead lettuce) every few weeks.

Planting

Though all crops have specific needs and requirements and there are nuances to cultivating each one, some guidelines apply to them all. The best practices below should give your plants—whether started from seed or purchased as transplants—a healthy foundation. (Much like raising young people, plants do best with consistency. Stress from an early age will ultimately affect their growth and resilience.)

BEST PRACTICES

• Plant for the season and specific microclimate, choosing varieties that are suited to both.

• Carefully integrate amendments into the top 8 inches (20 cm) of soil with a fork or trowel. Take care not to completely invert the soil; bringing everything up from the bottom to the top can damage the soil biology you are trying to cultivate. (For more on amending your soil, including using fertilizers, see page 181.)

• Evenly spread your amended soil to create a flat surface, breaking up large clumps. This will allow for even distribution of water.

• Plant in moist soil. If the area wasn't being regularly watered prior to planting, water the day before or at least a few hours in advance—but take care not to overdo it, as you don't want the soil to be too wet.

• Plant along your drip irrigation lines, if you have them. We like to position our irrigation lines in rows approximately 8 inches (20 cm) apart.

• Be mindful of adjacencies when planting. Locate plants where they have enough sunlight, space, nutrients, and water to thrive. Tomatoes, for example, may grow to a height that blocks the sun from lettuces planted below.

• Consider the depth. Don't bury seeds or transplants too deep or too shallow or leave roots exposed to air.

• Water immediately after planting, to ensure the seed and surrounding soil are moist. This also helps remove air pockets around the seed so that it has good soil contact.

• Label your crops (see page 210) so there is no confusion later as to what's what.

DIRECT SOWING

Some crops do better if they are grown directly from seed in the garden, as they struggle when their roots are disturbed during transplanting. These include hardy root vegetables such as carrots, radishes, and turnips. And for fast-growing plants like tender arugula, baby greens, cilantro, peas, and beans, it's easy (and cheaper!) to start them from seed rather than buy transplants. Here are some tips for sowing seeds directly in the ground.

• Seed in straight rows. If you have drip irrigation lines, quick greens and root crops can be seeded in a wide 3-inch (7.6 cm) band on both sides of the lines. This works especially well for arugula, baby lettuces, radishes, cilantro, and carrots. Plant larger crops in single file.

• For small seeds, like carrots and arugula, create a shallow (¼-inch/0.6 cm) furrow in your garden bed, parallel to the drip line (if using), and then sprinkle seeds along the furrow.

• When planting large seeds, including legumes and cucurbits, create a 1-inch-deep (2.5 cm) hole with your finger and place the seed inside. Alternatively, simply push the seed down to that depth into the soil with your fingertip.

• Certain seeds, such as corn and nasturtium, require an extra step prior to planting, such as soaking in water, stratification (cold treatment), or scarification (scratching the outer layer with a file or sandpaper, to soften or break down the seed coat). Check the seed packets for these details.

• Cover the seeds gently with soil. Pat down to make sure they are in contact with the soil and not in an air pocket, to ensure that watering doesn't wash them out of place.

• Label each row, listing both the crop name and the seeding date. This enables you to monitor the germination time and keep up with successions and harvests.

• Water gently, using a shower or mist setting on your hose, to avoid disturbing the seedbed and keep the soil moist until seeds have sprouted.

• Some seeded crops, especially radishes, carrots, and beets, need thinning after sprouting to allow enough room for each plant to reach full size. To thin, remove sprouts as necessary to allow one or two fingers' width between plants.

TRANSPLANTING

To get a head start on the growing season, you can propagate your seeds indoors or buy seedlings from a local nursery rather than wait the additional weeks (or even months) for warm-enough conditions to direct-seed in the ground. One advantage of growing plants from seeds is that you will have more plant varieties to choose from than what is available at your local nursery—it's also the less expensive option, particularly for larger spaces.

Because seeds can be started indoors earlier, when outside temperatures are still low, these transplants will be more mature at the beginning of the growing season, meaning they'll have more time to produce harvests before cold weather sets in again in fall. This comes in handy if you're in an area with shorter growing seasons, and is most useful for tomatoes, peppers, eggplants, broccoli, cabbage, and celery. Transplanting long-term crops is also useful in small spaces, freeing up weeks or months when garden space can be used more efficiently.

Knowing when a plant is ready to go outside varies by the type of plant and by the growing region. Generally speaking, seedlings should have two or three sets of "true leaves" before they are transferred outside. (The first leaves that appear after germination are called seed leaves, which aren't as efficient at photosynthesis as more mature leaves.) Seed packets will usually include guidelines for transplanting, as will the labels on nursery plants. Here are some additional pointers for planting seedlings.

• To ease shock, "bottom water" your seedlings prior to transplanting: Place their grow pots in a plastic container or tray filled with ½ inch (1.3 cm) of water and some liquid kelp (2 to 4 tablespoons should suffice, depending on the size of the container or tray). Let sit for one hour, or until most of the liquid has been soaked up.

• Another important measure to prevent shock is to avoid planting in high heat. Early in the morning, or on an overcast day, is best.

• To remove a plant from its pot, squeeze the bottom of the container to loosen the roots, and then gently pull with your other hand from the base of the plant. Gently tease apart the roots before planting.

• It's best to avoid plants that are root-bound (meaning the roots have formed a dense mat in the shape of the container); consider replacing with a younger seedling.

• Install plants at the same soil level as they grew in their container. The exceptions are tomatoes, which you plant deeper so that they develop extra roots along the stems, and leeks and green onions, which should be planted deeper so that they develop long stems.

• Water as soon as possible after planting; check the soil moisture 3 inches (7.6 cm) deep, to make sure water has reached the root zone.

SPACING

To receive the adequate sunlight, nutrients, water, and air required to thrive and produce at their best, plants need space. Typically, crops that grow relatively fast (under two months from seed or transplant to harvest) require less room. For the most prolific harvest, follow the spacing guidelines below.

Plant	Ideal Spacing
Arugula, carrots, cilantro, loose-leaf lettuces, radishes, turnips	20 to 40 seeds per linear foot (31 cm)
Beans, beets, mustard greens, peas, spinach	3 to 4 inches (8 to 10 cm)
Bok choy, endive, fennel, garlic, leeks, head lettuces, onions	6 to 10 inches (15 to 25 cm)
Basil, celery, chard, collards, kale, peppers, potatoes, strawberries	1 foot (30.5 cm)
Broccoli, cabbage, cauliflower, cucumber, eggplant	1½ feet (46 cm)
Squash and tomatoes	2 to 3 feet (61 to 91 cm)

POINTERS
FOR PERENNIALS

Fruits, berries, woody herbs, and any other perennial plant (edible or not) will grow for many years and therefore have slightly different needs than annual vegetables. In general, perennials are best planted directly in the ground, with plenty of room for their root systems to get well established (although some can grow happily in pots and planters).

It is recommended to plant these in early spring, while they're dormant or just beginning to waken. Because this season is typically rainy, the ground is soft and saturated, which makes the transition to the garden less stressful for the plants. For best results, follow these suggestions:

• Choose a location with sufficient sunlight and enough space for the plant to mature to full size.

• Dig a hole twice as wide and half as deep as the grow pot.

• Mix compost or nutrient-dense soil into the native soil you dug out so that you have a 50/50 mix (you can also apply any necessary fertilizers at this time, such as acidic fertilizer for blueberries).

• Fill the hole with water and let it absorb into the soil (if your soil is already wet, skip this step).

• Gently remove the plant from its pot, rolling it and pressing from the side to loosen the bottom roots before pulling it out. (Don't be afraid to break a few smaller roots; this will encourage new growth.)

• Place the plant in the hole, ensuring that the top of the plant's root-ball sits just below the level of the soil you are planting in.

• Backfill around the plant with the 50/50 mix of soil you just made (see third bullet) and any amendments, and then gently pat down to remove air pockets.

• Water immediately after planting; you want to make sure the soil is evenly moist around the plant and that the water has reached the roots.

Harvesting

How you harvest your crops is just as important as how you cultivate them. Each edible plant has an ideal harvesting window when it tastes its best, and some windows are wider than others. The best way to learn the look and feel of ripe produce, in all its varietal differences, is by taste-testing it. No matter what you're picking, the following advice should help you understand how to harvest when the time comes.

• Don't hesitate to harvest when the food's ready, even if you're not ready to eat it! Fruit left too long on the branch will get watery and seedy, and the flavor will be compromised. Leafy greens left too long grow tough, bitter, or overly spicy, and the plants will start to go to flower (this is called bolting; see page 177).

• Make sure plants are adequately watered before harvesting; dehydrated plants wilt faster and will not keep nearly as long as well-watered ones.

• Use sharp, sanitized clippers, scissors, or a knife to make clean cuts. Avoid tearing or tugging on the plants.

• For leafy greens with a long harvest window, such as kale and chard, pick from the outside of the plant, retaining four or five good leaves in the center so that the plant can continue to grow.

• Harvest leafy greens like arugula, chard, collards, kale, lettuce, spinach, and herbs in the coolness of the morning or evening, and immediately wash or dunk them in cold water to maintain peak texture and flavor. Shake off excess moisture or blot dry before storing.

• Clean the harvest before storage, removing dirt, pests, and any yellow or dried-out leaves. Move inside and, depending on the variety, refrigerate as soon as possible (see below for guidelines on ideal storage).

WHERE TO STORE YOUR HARVEST

Space	Produce
Countertop (away from light and heat)	Avocados, basil (place upright in a glass with 1 inch/2.5 cm of water), eggplant, garlic, melon, onions, potatoes, tomatoes, winter squash
Fridge	Asparagus, berries, broccoli, Brussels sprouts, cabbage, carrots, cauliflower, cilantro, corn, dark leafy greens, grapes, leeks, lettuce, parsley, peas, summer squash/zucchini
Countertop to ripen, fridge once ripe	Most fruit

❶ 'Hot Streak' and 'Marnouar' tomatoes, and 'Snow White' cherry tomatoes. ❷ 'Sora' red radishes, kales, bok choy, and spinach. ❸ 'Hansel' eggplant, 'Dragon's Tongue' beans, 'Red of Florence' onion, 'Diva' cucumber, and limes. ❹ 'Dark Red Norland' and 'Magic Molly' purple potatoes.

Styling the Harvest

Despite all best efforts, putting fresh, flavorful produce to immediate use is sometimes impossible, especially in a bumper-crop season. In those cases, I suggest turning to some time-honored techniques for extending the life of your garden bounty: freezing, dehydrating, canning, and pickling. But I also encourage you to transform some of the excess harvest into gifts and decor, to show off the well-earned fruits of your labor. Here are a few of my favorite ways to do so.

CORNUCOPIA BOUQUET

There's nothing better than the feeling of sharing a harvest basket of homegrown produce with neighbors and friends. The only downside is having to ask for the basket itself back, or worse yet, worrying you'll never see it again! This harvest bouquet is the perfect solution, making it easy to arrange a beautiful gift of fruits and vegetables, without having to part with any of your favorite containers.

❶ Harvest and clean whatever produce is at its peak in the garden. Cut a large square of parchment or butcher paper and lay it out in a diamond shape, with one corner pointing away from you.

❷ Place the largest leaves (such as kale, chard, or collards) flat on the paper so they cover the top corner. The bottom stems should end three-quarters of the way down the square, with the bottom corner of the paper uncovered. Trim stems with clippers if necessary.

❸ Keep layering on more vegetables and herbs, tapering them along the edges to mirror the V of the paper. Root vegetables look best placed with tips up. Vegetables without long stems (such as zucchini, eggplant, or peppers) can be nestled toward the base where the paper will soon encircle them. Once your produce is arranged, fold the left and right corners of the paper in until they just touch the vegetables.

❹ Carefully fold the bottom corner of the paper up over the stems, then fold the left and right sides over the bottom corner and hold firmly in place. Secure the bundle with twine or a ribbon. To complete the look, adorn with edible flowers.

BRAIDED GARLIC

My favorite way to store garlic after harvesting is in a decorative braid that makes my pantry feel homestead-worthy (and helps the garlic last longer than when bundled in a bag with no airflow). Braiding is easiest with softneck garlic, but because I prefer hardneck varieties, I've included one simple step that works for both types.

To prepare your freshly harvested garlic for braiding, let it cure for a few days by leaving it to dry in a shady, well-ventilated space until the outer layers are papery but the stem is still pliable. Then, brush off any dirt, prune the roots, and strip off any dried leaves. If you're using a hardneck variety, lay the garlic flat and carefully slit the outer layers with the tip of sharp clippers or a knife to expose and remove the inner stem (remember that the outer layers need to stay intact for braiding). Then follow the steps below to complete your braid. You can add a little flair by weaving in dried herbs or flowers.

❶ Lay three heads of garlic parallel to one another on your work surface, with the two side stems overlapping the central stem.

❷ One at a time, wrap the overlapping stems under and around the central stem until they are both on top, facing down and aligned with the main stem. Hold tight with one hand.

❸ Add three more heads of garlic in the same manner, with the middle one first, then the other two tucked in on the sides. Again, wrap the new overlapping/side stems under the newly added heads of garlic and back down the front.

❹ Repeat the steps until you have a beautifully formed braid. Tie the top tightly with twine and create a loop for hanging. Hang the garlic braid somewhere where you can admire it (ideally, in a cool place, out of direct sunlight) and store it for months. Cut off the garlic heads as needed.

HERB WREATH

An herb wreath is the perfect way to celebrate the variety of flavors in your garden. In addition to fresh herbs, the wreath can be adorned with fresh or dried flowers, heads of garlic, or chile peppers. You can experiment from season to season with whatever you find in the garden and the surrounding landscape—budding branches in spring, tufts of dried grass in fall, and so on. Freshly harvested herbs with sturdy stems, such as rosemary and bay leaves, work best. More delicate herbs should be dried upside down for a few days first so that their stems dry straight.

❶ Purchase a wreath base, or easily create one by bending a grapevine, a willow branch, or thick wire into a round approximately 8 inches (20 cm) in diameter. Gather your herbs, approximately twenty to forty of each (depending on the size and variety), keeping the long stems intact and in separate piles arranged in front of you. Twist one end of the floral wire around the base circle until secure (this is where you'll start attaching your herbs).

❷ Select a handful of herbs from the first pile to your left, and place them over the floral wire. Loop the floral wire around the stems a few times to fasten the herbs to the base. Now gather a bundle from the second variety and place it just below the previous one, with the tops of the greenery covering the stems and wire of the previous bundle. Loop the floral wire around the new stems to attach. Be sure to use enough herbs to hide the wreath base when viewed from the side or inside of the circle, adding more individual stems as needed.

❸ Repeat the process from step 2, selecting bundles of herbs in the same order to create a repeating pattern, until you've covered the whole base in a patchwork of herbs.

❹ Tuck and secure the last bundle under the tips of the first to complete the circle. Gently flip the wreath over, cut the tail end of the floral wire and pass it under an earlier loop of wire, twisting the end back on itself to fasten. If desired, add a loop in the wire for hanging.

Equipment Guide

As with all things food forward, I aim for function *and* beauty when it comes to tools. I encourage you to do the same. Upgrade the everyday equipment, care for it properly, and keep it within easy, orderly reach, so that no garden task ever seems like a grind. Opt for durability and style, and avoid flimsy or single-use items as much as you can. You'll find that doesn't require a large quiver of tools, so long as you stick with time-tested essentials.

I feel more connected to tools and accessories that have a story behind them, which is why I go out of my way to support local artisans and search for antique pieces to add to my collection. Harvesting the fruits of your garden labor in a beautiful woven basket, pruning with Japanese steel, or decorating with unique plant labels further elevates the entire experience. More of a joy, less of a chore.

A Look Inside My Tool Kit

Much like a purse or wallet, a tool kit is a reflection of its owner. My goal is to always strike the right balance between including anything I might require, and not packing in so much that it becomes cumbersome to carry and difficult to keep tidy. Over time, your tool kit will no doubt be fine-tuned to match your personal preferences and needs. Below are my essentials, followed by a few more lists of helpful accessories for any number of garden situations.

❶ **Harvest Knife** When harvesting lettuce, cabbage, broccoli, and asparagus, among other crops, it's best to cut them off at the base or shear off just above the soil surface. Any small paring knife will do, but if you want one specifically for the garden, I suggest one with a serrated blade or a folding handle, which can be slipped into a pocket.

❷ **Clippers** I never go into the garden without sharp cutting tools, one sturdy pair *(bottom)* for pruning out larger, woody stems and a needle-nose pair *(top)* for more delicate, tender stems like pea shoots.

❸ **Gloves** Find a pair of gloves that are comfortable and fit you well, retaining enough dexterity to operate clippers and the like without constantly taking them on and off. I've tried many styles, and the ones I keep coming back to are formfitting, water resistant just on the palm, breathable on top, and securely elasticized around the wrist so they don't fill up with dirt. It's okay to have multiple pairs for different tasks—if you have roses or other prickly pruning jobs, leather gloves with longer sleeves are a no-brainer.

❹ **Seeds** Admittedly not a tool, seed packets are a tool kit essential nonetheless. By keeping a small supply of seeds on hand, you help ensure a continuous supply of fresh vegetables in season. This is primarily important for direct-sown crops that are planted multiple times throughout the season for succession harvests (especially the faster-return crops like radishes, Japanese turnips, arugula, and other loose-leaf salad greens—and, in summer, beans). For more on growing edibles from seed, see page 192.

❺ **Holster** The garden is the Wild West, and you don't want to be caught unaware. More important, you don't want to be setting your clippers down and losing them between the leaves.

❻ **Twine** This comes in handy for too many garden tasks to mention. Rest assured you'll reach for twine when tying plants to their trellises, securing harvest bundles, and hanging herbs to dry, among myriad other uses.

❼ **Hori Hori** My favorite garden tool of all, a hori hori (which roughly translates to "dig dig") is an all-in-one Japanese-style trowel with a knife edge of sorts. Use it for removing old plants and cutting through roots, digging holes for planting, and much more. Look for a hori hori with a full-tang metal hilt with wood siding (rather than an attached handle, which is likely to break off); measuring markers along the blade front are also helpful.

SUNDRIES

A few other essential supplies that never leave the kit: sunscreen, permanent marker (for labeling), scissors (for cutting twine or row cover cloth), clipper sharpener, irrigation staples and extra irrigation pieces for fixing leaks (connectors and plugs of varying sizes), and measuring cup and spoons (for fertilizers and concentrates). A small spray bottle of disinfectant is useful for cleaning hands and tools to avoid spreading disease.

Harvest Baskets

Baskets are like hats, shoes, or cakes—you can never have too many! I enjoy keeping a collection on hand so I can choose whichever strikes my fancy or fits the shape and quantity of the day's bounty. Every one of the regulars listed below is in use during the peak fall harvest and other busy times of year.

❶ Forager Basket Whether you're mushroom hunting or apple scrumping, the key to comfortable foraging is having a lightweight yet deep basket with a sturdy shoulder strap.

❷ Wooden Trug A versatile tray-shaped basket with shallow sides, the trug is ideal for delicate produce such as leafy greens, tomatoes, and flowers that can't tolerate stacking.

❸ Small Lidded Baskets A pair of these comes in handy for gathering delicate edible flowers and storing seed packets.

❹ Metal Basket One of the best things about durable metal baskets is that they can double as colanders for washing vegetables. Simply spray off the dirt with a hose while you are outside.

❺ Willow Basket Bushel baskets are the most practical choice for large harvests, while shallow trays make easy work of collecting lettuces, large tomatoes, and summer squash, all of which need room to breathe to avoid crushing or bruising them.

❻ Market Basket Hand-woven, durable straw baskets like this one can be put to frequent use. They are ideal for delivering produce to friends and family.

❼ All-Weather Basket A robust, heavy-duty basket like this New England-style garden hod holds up to most environments. The wire mesh is coated with food-grade PVC. Use it to harvest potatoes, small fruits, and flowers.

❽ Berry Basket To keep delicate produce from bruising, use small containers, and avoid stacking them. These are ideal for berries of all kinds, as well as for cherry tomatoes. You can find them made from wood or recycled paper, and even ceramic versions.

Labels

Even the most experienced gardener can't be expected to remember each and every variety they've planted. This is especially true when growing from seeds: Use labels to mark the spot until the seedlings germinate and make themselves known. Keeping track of specific varieties will also help you identify new favorites and hone your planting plan each season.

Labels also present a simple, fairly inexpensive opportunity for garden "accessorizing." Get creative with labels that fit your style. Remember to include the planting date for seeded crops, in case germination is slow; this will also come in handy as you plan succession plantings.

❶ **Wire Hook and Tag** In some cases, I prefer markers on tall metal stands so that they peek above the foliage rather than getting lost on the ground plane. For the hanging tag, there are multiple shapes and materials to choose from; metal and slate (pictured here) are my favorites.

❷ **Wood** Wooden plant labels are easy to procure in a variety of sizes. Some last longer than others, depending on the variety and thickness of the wood; cedar, redwood, and oak (pictured here) are good options. You can use Popsicle sticks, too. Mark with a permanent marker or waterproof paint pen.

❸ **Copper** Bright and versatile, copper labels can be marked with a permanent marker or embossed: To do the latter, place the copper label on a soft surface (like a tea towel) and write firmly with a ballpoint pen or dull pencil to etch the shape of each letter. Copper labels with a hole punched are a good choice for tying to tree trunks.

❹ **Slate** Slate labels are a timeless, old-world classic. They look especially at home in stone-walled garden beds or pots. Use with a white waterproof chalk marker.

❺ **Stamped Silverware** Mismatched silverware (spoons and butter knives work best) embossed with block lettering are great for labeling plants in pots and herb plots. You can find these prestamped on craft sites, or do it yourself with an embossing kit.

The Potting Bench

Think of the potting bench as the outdoor equivalent to a well-organized kitchen, where instead of turning ingredients into meals, you're starting the seeds that will become your ingredients. Aim to create an orderly, ergonomic, well-stocked space where you can tackle the first steps of growing food. I highly recommend borrowing a technique from the French kitchen known as *mise en place*. It means "putting in place," or gathering everything you need before you begin: your ingredients prepped and measured, knives sharpened, sturdy pots and pans within reach. In the garden, you'll want to keep your plants, soil amendments, and tools close by. Set aside room for dry storage of perishables (fertilizers and seeds) as well as for labels, seeds, twine, and such in receptacles on the bench. Most important, ensure you've left sufficient countertop space for cleaning your harvest, potting up seeds, and braiding garlic bulbs (see page 200), among any number of seasonal endeavors.

This extra effort to get prepared at the outset will go a long way toward making your time in the garden more rewarding. Instead of dashing back and forth, you can focus on the tasks at hand and get into the quiet rhythm of the garden. Find inspiration for your own workstation on the following page, by taking a closer look at the components of my custom potting bench.

ANATOMY OF A POTTING BENCH

A potting bench can take many forms. Whether it's a simple repurposed side table or custom-built cabinetry, the function remains largely the same: to act as a hub for organized, productive gardening, with everything in view rather than tucked away in the garage or shed.

A streamlined workstation is more than just the sum of its parts. I designed my bench at home, pictured here, for the most efficient workflow and easiest cleanup. Garden tasks generally start on the left, where the sink (the first stop for harvested vegetables) is located, and finish near the compost chute on the far end. Below are the core building blocks of my setup.

❶ **Wash Station** A sink is without a doubt the most utilitarian addition to any potting bench, endlessly useful for washing hands, tools, fresh-picked harvests, and more. I keep a variety of brushes sinkside for scrubbing dirt-covered root crops (and fingernails). To help ensure that no drop goes to waste, gray water is used to irrigate fruit trees nearby.

❷ **Drying Rack** Air drying is an easy, low-effort way to preserve food, and having a dedicated spot to hang herbs, flowers, and chile peppers makes it wonderfully convenient. Here, bundles of marigolds, amaranth, and lavender are suspended from the shade awning, but string or wire that runs flush against a wall would work just as well. The only requirements are ample airflow around the cut plants and low humidity. To help the plants retain color while they dry, keep them out of direct sunlight. Fruits and vegetables with higher moisture content, such as figs and tomatoes, are more suitable to drying once sliced and laid flat in the sunshine but can also be strung on a line to hang dry.

❸ **Seed Station** As its name implies, a potting bench serves primarily as a space for planting seeds and seedlings into pots or trays before they're ready to go into the ground. For easy cleanup, I keep an under-counter drawer stocked with seed-starting mix; after filling a few trays or pots, any excess soil is quickly swept back into the bin.

❹ **Prep Counter** The countertop is where I write labels, measure fertilizers, gather my tools, and pack up produce before taking it into the kitchen. Make sure to position it at a comfortable height, to keep from having to bend over while you work.

❺ **Compost Chute** A built-in green waste disposal minimizes the time and effort spent walking to the compost pile. It can be as simple as a cut-out in the countertop with a large bin hidden from sight in the cabinet below.

❻ **Dry Storage** Storage space below the bench allows you to keep fertilizer, baskets, seeds, hand tools, and other necessities protected from the elements yet still close to the garden. Cabinets and drawers keep the potting bench looking clutter-free.

Part IV

THE PLANTS

Sixty-Plus Tried-and-True Edibles

THE LISTS THAT FOLLOW ARE DESIGNED TO SERVE
as a jumping-off point for your own food forward gardens. They
include the plants I rely on most to create my projects. All are
widely available and relatively easy to grow in a range of climate
zones. Before you decide on a single plant, however, get to know the
nuanced environmental conditions of your region and specifically
your yard. From there, it pays to start small, with species that are
more hands-off and forgiving. After a season (or better yet, two),
when you've learned which plants thrive (or not) in your garden, you
can move on to new additions and start to introduce less-familiar
yet equally delicious specialty varieties.

Herbs

The herbs listed below are sturdy enough to hold their own among ornamentals, and pretty enough to blend right in. Plant these in full sun, close to the kitchen. All herbs benefit from regular pruning, which encourages fresh growth and keeps them more tender, fragrant, and at their peak flavor.

❶ Basil Basil ranks as one of my favorite herbs. It's a focal point of the summer garden and a fun filler in bouquets. 'Prospera' is my go-to variety for giant batches of pesto, and it's also more disease resistant than other varieties. 'Dark Opal' basil looks stunning within a sea of green summer growth and adds moody visual interest on the plate as well.

❷ Bay Laurel Every landscape I design comes with a lifetime supply of bay leaves. In addition to its culinary uses, this versatile plant is excellent as a low-water evergreen hedge, filler, or screening plant that can be left to grow tall and bushy, or kept clipped. The ovate leaves are a lovely dark shade of olive green, and, of course, they smell fantastic.

❸ Chives These members of the onion family hold a special place in my heart. Their form and grace—and their purple pom-pom puffball flowers—stand out in any garden. I love to frame a central pathway or other view line, like the front corners of two adjacent raised beds, with chives. Don't miss the chance to sprinkle the petals on salads, eggs, toasts, and everything in between.

❹ Marjoram A subspecies of oregano, marjoram has a milder, more delicate flavor and a more upright growth habit. It doesn't spread as aggressively as oregano, yet it tends to flower more often. Try using marjoram to flavor butternut squash soup or pasta dishes. The plant also has an array of medicinal properties.

❺ Oregano Part of the mint family, oregano is an aggressive spreading herb with low-mounding stalks that eventually grow a few inches (6 to 8 cm) tall and produce tiny white flowers. Avoid planting oregano in a small pot with other plants, as it will eventually crowd them out. Its rambling appearance complements stone pathways and walls.

❻ Rosemary Rosemary is the workhorse of the herb world and thus my absolute favorite (don't tell the others). This is partly due to size (some species can reach 4 feet/1.2 m) but mainly because it's reliably low maintenance and flexible. You can use rosemary as a low hedge, a topiary, a potted focal point, or a dark green backdrop for other plants. Its light blue flowers are some of the earliest bloomers each year, making it a useful food source for pollinators.

❼ Sage Culinary sages include silver, green, and purple varieties. Their large ovate leaves and upright growth habit make them ideal candidates as accent plants, with silvery foliage that provides excellent contrast against other greens. If you're lucky, your sage plants will send up spires of purplish flowers toward the end of summer. True to its Mediterranean nature, sage grows best in arid conditions, so avoid overwatering.

❽ Tarragon I use tarragon sparingly in cooking (though it's delicious with chicken and in creamy salad dressings), but that doesn't stop me from planting it profusely. It's among the most beautiful culinary herbs, with slim, feathery leaves that adorn long, graceful stems. Tarragon looks especially lovely when it trails over the sides of raised beds or pots. Unlike other perennial herbs, tarragon will go dormant during winter and won't be visible until it sprouts back up in spring.

❾ Thyme While I love creeping thyme that spans the gap between paving stones, the culinary varieties—English, French, and lemon—grow into bushy mounds that trail beautifully over the corners of raised beds and containers or along the edge of a planting bed. English varieties of thyme tend to form a denser shape than their slender-leaved French counterparts. Enjoy their fragrant, edible flower buds (white, pink, or purple) in spring.

Aromatics

There's nothing quite so comforting as a tea garden. Call them what you will, the following edible aromatics are powerhouses of flavor, just waiting to be steeped into sun tea, dried for hot teas and medicinal tinctures, or used fresh in all sorts of culinary applications. Luckily, it's easy to incorporate these plants into flower beds, herb pots, and everywhere in between.

❶ **Chamomile** The low-growing Roman (or English) chamomile, a great ground cover in cottage gardens, and the taller German variety, which produces a comparatively prolific number of small flowers, both make excellent teas. I prefer the latter for mixing into flower and vegetable beds, since its slender stems blend in well with the cutting flowers.

❷ **Hops** Hops are fast-growing vines that will twine their way up any cable or trellis (as high as 25 feet/7.6 m, in a single season!). They are perfect for greening up walls or fences or providing summer shade over arbors and seating areas. Hops cones can be harvested in fall, and are great for tea, especially sipped just before bed.

❸ **Lavender** Is there anything that lavender can't do? This plant is so versatile; it could easily be included on our lists of favorite herbs, edible flowers, and favorite pollinators. With a wide range of colors and sizes, lavender can be grown as an accent flower, a border hedge, or a potted specimen. Once harvested, dry the blossoms as an aromatic to use as a sleep aid or to perfume every room; just place it in bowls or sachets, or mix it into bath salts and sugar scrubs. It also has multiple culinary uses: in drinks (like lemonade), desserts (pair it with honey to flavor ice cream), dry rubs, and more.

❹ **Lemon Balm** Marked by bright green, ruffled leaves, this member of the mint family is best grown in pots and planters. Its lemon flavor is milder than that of lemon verbena or lemongrass; as a tea, it is touted for its calming effects.

❺ **Lemongrass** Hailing from tropical climes, lemongrass is easy to grow in many nontropical zones, too, as long as it's protected from frost in winter. (If you live in a zone that gets frost, a good workaround is to grow it in pots and bring it indoors when the weather gets cold.) Lemongrass will quickly grow bushy, like a big clumping ornamental grass, and might go unrecognized as an edible species were it not for its deliciously fragrant stalks.

❻ **Lemon Verbena** This vigorous branching shrub, with bright green foliage and a spray of pale pink to white flowers in late summer, makes a standout addition to ornamental or vegetable gardens (and an unbeatable tea). In cold climates, it's an annual that never quite reaches full size.

❼ **Mint** Did you know there are more than six hundred mint varieties, each with its own distinct flavor profile? Try peppermint, chocolate mint, apple mint, spearmint, or pineapple mint in teas, mixed drinks, or chutneys. Get adventurous—just remember to keep this aggressive spreader contained in pots and planters, unless you want it roaming across your yard with abandon.

❽ **Stevia** You've likely heard of stevia as a sugar substitute, but did you know that it's easy to grow? Native to South America, this bushy green plant has leaves that resemble a cross between sage and marjoram. It's grown as a perennial in warm climates but as an annual in cooler zones. Use one or two fresh leaves to sweeten a cup of tea; once dried, the leaves can be ground to a powder to use in cooking or baking.

❾ **Tulsi** Often referred to as holy basil, tulsi is a powerful medicinal herb revered for its immune-enhancing and stress-modulating properties. It's best grown in pots or raised beds, as you would grow common basil.

Edible Flowers

I consider it a win-win when flowers are at once beautiful *and* distinctly flavorful. Let this list inspire a whole new palette of color and texture in your garden—and on your dinner plate. In addition to the species below, any flowering herb (such as cilantro and chives) or vegetable (including kale, broccoli, radish, and squash, among others) is fair game.

❶ Bachelor's Button Also known as cornflowers, these vibrant blue (or occasionally white, pink, or purple) blooms on slender stalks are perfect for interplanting with tall crops like corn, weaving among trellises with vining plants, or lending a whimsical prairie look to tall grass meadows.

❷ Borage Borage is a cottage-garden dream come true, a bushy plant with large pale gray fuzzy leaves and stunning star-shaped pale blue flowers. Bees adore them, as do I—in and out of the garden (they taste, surprisingly, of cucumber). The plants can get large and readily self-seed, so plant them in the corners of your garden or along flower borders.

❸ Calendula A powerful medicinal plant, calendula is easy to grow and brightens up any garden with its big, daisylike blooms, which come in bright orange, yellow, and (my favorite) pale strawberry blonde. Introduce calendula in raised beds or as part of a meadow or cottage-style planting scheme. With regular deadheading, it will continue to flower tirelessly. Pluck the petals off and toss them into salads, or use them as an ingredient in healing beeswax salves.

❹ Carnation Due to their wide range of bright colors and festive frills, carnations (or dianthus) are as fun as edible decorations as they are in flower arrangements (and high-school dance boutonnieres). Despite the blossoms' delicate appearance, carnation plants are surprisingly drought tolerant, with silvery green stems that look wonderful in rock gardens.

❺ Marigold These quintessential late-summer and autumn flowers are edible, and also help protect your vegetables from pests. Their strong smell is a deterrent to unwanted insects, so plant them around the perimeter of your garden to act as security guards.

❻ Nasturtium A secret weapon in the vegetable garden, nasturtium is an excellent "trap crop," meaning it attracts aphids, keeping your other plants free of pests. Both the large flowers and round leaves of nasturtiums are edible, with a distinctly peppery flavor. This fast-growing vine drapes beautifully over retaining walls and slopes, and it can tolerate some shade.

❼ Rose My favorite rose varieties are those with open centers, such as sweetbriars (pictured). They most resemble wild roses' perfect, unpretentious beauty. These varieties also happen to be the best for producing rose hips, which (along with the petals) have endless creative culinary uses.

❽ Stock These spirelike ruffled flowers come in a range of pastel colors with a ubiquitous nostalgic perfume. Because stock is in the brassica family, the petals have a subtle peppery flavor, similar to a radish. This makes them a great choice for salads, but they can also be candied and used to adorn sweets. Similar to its vegetable relatives, stock prefers the mild temperatures of spring over the blazing heat of summer.

❾ Viola and Pansy The cheerful faces of these flowers are my go-to garnishes for baked goods, and they come in almost any color you can imagine. The fuss-free edible flowers are perfect for partial-shade areas and look great hanging over the edges of garden beds.

Pollinator Species

I recommend planting a mix of flower types to satisfy a variety of pollinators. Tubular flowers with deep nectar reserves are perfect for hummingbirds, while flattop blooms and small flower clusters are great for butterflies and bees. Color is also a factor: Bees are drawn to blues and purples, while butterflies prefer reds and pinks. The following are pollinator species that grow well in a range of climate zones. Most are perennials, best incorporated into in-ground planting areas.

❶ African Blue Basil African blue basil is the only tender perennial on this list (it won't tolerate frost). This variety gets much bushier than standard culinary basil and produces a nonstop profusion of flowers that are absolute bee magnets. It also smells heavenly and makes a wonderful addition to flower arrangements. I include this plant in every vegetable garden or orchard possible, to add symmetry or frame pathways and steps. African blue basil must be propagated from cuttings and can be difficult to find, but if you come across some plants for sale, buy them all.

❷ Anise Hyssop With a slightly sweet, licorice-like flavor, anise hyssop is often brewed to make tea (which aids in digestion), or steeped into syrups to flavor desserts. Once cut, the long-lasting flowers bring beautiful color and height to arrangements.

❸ Bergamot Bergamot (or bee balm) could just as easily be on the edible or aromatic plant lists. Its tufted flower spikes appeal not only to bees but also to hummingbirds and other pollinators. A distant relative of mint, it is best planted somewhere where it can spread and grow tall. I like to place it next to Agastache and echinacea. Its

blooms are white, pink, dark red, lavender, or purple, depending on the variety.

❹ Catmint This prolific performer is equally at home in cottage-style gardens as it is in minimalist modern landscapes and everywhere in between. My favorite ways to use it are spilling over pathways, planted in drifts among grasses, and softening the sharp outlines of topiary globes and other rigid architectural structures by adding a little whimsy.

❺ Ceanothus This pollinator establishes itself nicely in the garden, filling in unsightly bare spaces with glossy green leaves and early-blooming blue flowers.

❻ Echinacea The quintessential prairie flower, echinacea (or coneflower) makes an eye-catching addition to tall grasses and mixed borders. When a planting scheme is missing a focal flower to stand out among the greens and tans, consider echinacea. I'm partial to the 'White Swan' variety (pictured), but the classic pinkish purple type is stunning in the right circumstances. It has both edible and medicinal applications, and makes for a wonderful tea.

❼ Salvia I like a number of salvia varieties, including *Salvia nemorosa* (pictured), *Salvia clevelandii*, and *Salvia spathacea*, though there are many more species to explore, in an array of colors and sizes. Their upright flower sprigs create contrast against flowing grasses or rambling herbs like catmint and are excellent at attracting hummingbirds. The larger specimens and low-spreading varieties can be quite drought tolerant.

❽ *Teucrium chamaedrys* Among pollinators, teucrium is quickly becoming as indispensable as lavender in our garden designs. In fact, the dark green foliage and rosy pink flowers of teucrium complement the silver and purple of lavender extremely well. Its low shape makes it a good candidate for bordering pathways and steps or breaking up swaths of golden grasses.

❾ Yarrow With so many flower colors and tones to explore, there is a yarrow to fit every garden, even a drought-tolerant one. Its flower heads provide plenty of space for pollinators to make themselves comfortable, and the lacy foliage and flat clusters of tiny flowers make eye-catching additions to cutting gardens.

Annuals (Vegetables)

While all vegetables are welcome in my garden, this group has garnered my everlasting admiration and increasingly large proportions of growing space in our raised beds. What sets them apart? All are forgiving—easy to grow and requiring little maintenance, with long harvest windows (meaning they can wait until the weekend). Naturally, they all taste (and look) great, too.

❶ Beets Although beets are part of the spinach and chard family (as you can tell from their tasty green tops), their growth and care are similar to carrots and the rest of the root crops. Best grown from seed in spring and fall, beets are prized for their earthy flavor, and I enjoy planting golden, deep red, and specialty striped 'Chioggia' varieties.

❷ Carrots There is something quite satisfying about tugging a bright orange carrot out of the ground with a small *pop* and taking a sweet, crunchy bite. This is a whole different experience than eating the large, bagged carrots you'll find in stores, which are often dried out after spending weeks or even months in storage. (This adaptability for storing does make them a staple food source, however, much like potatoes. If this is what you're after, there are varieties specifically suited to that.) Carrots are best grown directly from seed, as an addition to the spring or fall garden (they don't love summer heat). The best part? You can harvest baby carrots while waiting for the rest to get bigger, thus extending the harvest window over many weeks. Be sure to thin young carrot seedlings so that each root has room to grow without crowding its neighbor. For added variety, try purple, yellow, white, or even pink carrots.

❸ Garlic To grow garlic requires, above all, patience. Planted in fall, each clove takes nine months to grow and divide into new fully formed heads of garlic (that's right, the gestation time is about the same as for humans). Aside from hogging garden space for such a long stretch, they are relatively unfussy and only ask three things of the gardener: adequate sun, food, and cold temperatures. It helps to supplement with nitrogen a few times during the growing period. Some of my favorite varieties include 'Music' (giant cloves), 'Chesnok Red' (known for its beautiful coloring), and 'Metechi' (for some spicy notes).

❹ Leeks My love for leeks—another stalwart English potager pick—is twofold. First, in the culinary arena, leeks are hard to beat for their comforting flavor. Second, the upright green stalks make a strong architectural statement in an otherwise leafy vegetable garden; in fact, a long row of leeks is one of my favorite design tricks.

❺ Peas True harbingers of spring, peas have delicate pale green tendrils reaching toward the sun, pure white blossoms, and slender, snappy pods that grow plump until it's time to harvest. They make the perfect snack as you wander through your garden rows. Like carrots and beets, peas are easy to grow from seed. My favorites are sugar peas, which can reach 6 feet (1.8 m) high, as well as snow peas and, of course, my beloved (nonmushy, please) English peas.

❻ Peppers As you might guess, peppers, especially hot ones such as Thai chiles (pictured), prefer sunny locations with lots of heat. My favorite variety to grow is shishito; these small, sweet frying peppers are adaptable to slightly cooler temperatures and are prolific producers. It's also convenient to have jalapeños on hand for summer salsas. I find that Italian roasting peppers (specifically the cultivars known as 'Carmen' and 'Lipstick') perform better than the juicier bell peppers, especially in more temperate climates.

❼ Radishes Sometimes you need a quick-and-easy win, which is right where radishes fit in. Most radishes go from seed to harvest in just four to six weeks, making them one of the fastest-growing crops. As they mature, harvest the largest ones first to make room for the rest to

grow round. Don't wait too long, though—radishes are the most time- and temperature-sensitive vegetables on this list and will get bitter and pithy if left in the ground too long.

❽ Tomatoes Many a garden has been built solely out of the desire for homegrown tomatoes—a just cause, in my opinion. The flavor is so vastly superior to anything you can buy at the store. Technically speaking, there are two types of tomatoes: determinate (with fruit that matures relatively all at the same time) and indeterminate (these continue flowering and fruiting throughout the season). Indeterminate varieties are usually the best choice for home gardeners, unless your primary goal is canning tomato sauce (in

which case opt for determinate paste tomatoes, so you can get one large harvest). Cherry tomatoes grow on rambunctious, far-reaching plants, making them right at home on archways and tall trellises. 'Sungold', 'Super Sweet 100', 'Chocolate Sprinkles', and 'Snow White' are my go-to cultivars. For larger tomatoes, I gravitate toward 'Hot Streak' (pictured on previous page), 'New Girl', 'Black Krim', 'Green Zebra', 'Pineapple', and 'Cherokee Purple', among many, many varieties. Although all tomatoes prefer as much sun as possible (eight to twelve or more hours, ideally), keep in mind that the larger the fruit, the more sun the plant will need.

❾ Winter Squash The ultimate plant-it-and-forget-it crop, winter

squash—including butternut, kabocha, spaghetti, acorn, and pumpkin—are planted in spring, grown all summer long, and harvested in late fall (where they last and last in the larder, providing sustenance and a sense of security well through the long winter). The trailing green vines and wide leaves can cover great distances, spreading out under taller crops or trailing over walls. As summer ends, the plump golden brown, orange, or dark green fruit harkens the transition to fall. I value their slow-and-steady approach to life and enjoy filling my kitchen with a variety of squashes that are in no rush to be eaten. Because they're so sturdy and long-lasting, they travel well and make nice homegrown gifts for friends and neighbors.

Berries

The ultimate foraging species, beloved by children and adults alike, berries remain top of mind when I'm designing interactive edible landscapes. Given their superstar status in the fruit world (and extravagant prices at the market), you might be surprised to realize how easy they are to grow. I encourage home gardeners to include as many berries from the list below as their square footage and climate will allow, then to stand back and watch the harvest baskets fill higher each year as these long-lived plants get established. As with other edibles, it pays to keep the smaller types near pathways, for easy access. Place the midsize bushes a little farther back into the bed (about 2 feet/0.5 m) and reserve the rambling kind for fence lines, arbors, or the wilder edges of your property.

❶ Alpine Strawberries None of my projects are complete without alpine strawberries somewhere in the planting plan. The berries add a playful, colorful element to pathway edges and border plantings, flowering for months on end. These miniature delicacies, known as *fraises des bois* (berries of the woods) in culinary circles, are packed with a unique flavor, distinct from the taste of market strawberries (more on these on page 234). They differ from wild ground cover strawberries in two key ways: They don't send out runners (in other words, they won't spread), and they grow taller, forming up to 9-inch (23 cm) high and wide vibrant light green mounds that add a welcome brightness to darker, partial shade areas.

❷ Blackberries Nothing captures the essence of summer quite like purple-stained fingertips from foraging for sweet blackberries on a hot day. Bring that feeling home by growing your own blackberry patch, but be sure to choose a variety without the same sting of thorns you may recall from your childhood brambles. There are now plenty of thornless cultivars available, and their flavor is undiminished. They still like to ramble, though, so grow them along a back fence or in a side yard, and do your best to keep them in check with regular pruning.

❸ Blueberries There are many categories of blueberry bushes, each with distinct characteristics and flavor profiles, but I tend to select the more compact varieties for the ornamental landscape— both 'Sunshine Blue' (pictured) and 'FLX-2' (sold as Bountiful Blue) fit the bill. I like how their silvery leaves provide contrast, and the way their pretty, pinkish white flowers appear in springtime. They look at home in nearly any landscape, and foragers of all ages seem to find the plump purple berries irresistible. Blueberries can be slightly fussy, with fertility needs and specific soil-balancing requirements (acidic soil works best), but they are well worth any extra TLC. As with many other fruiting species, it's always best to plant more than one variety, as cross-pollination increases production.

❹ Currants With their striking trusses of pink flowers in spring, currants are a worthwhile addition to your garden solely for their ornamental virtues. The maplelike shape of their leaves, which appear along upright canes (revealing their close relationship with blackberries and raspberries), adds a novel texture to planting beds. Currants are commonplace in England, and I admit to missing them when spring rolls around and I'm at home in California. The tart berries come in a range of hues, from white to darkest red/purple, and are delicious in jam, syrup, or homemade sorbet.

❺ Elderberries Elderberries are too astringent to eat fresh but have long been used for medicinal purposes, in addition to being distilled into syrup and wine. There is something about picking elderberries that calls to mind our foraging forebears. The tiny dark purple berries grow in clusters on large shrubs. Since the plants can get quite big, I prefer to include them along fence lines or toward the back of planting beds. Their frothy white flowers are some of the first spring blooms and can themselves be used for nearly as many recipes as the berries.

❻ Gooseberries Best suited to the cooler temperatures of the eastern US and northern Europe (they are a staple in England), gooseberries are rarely for sale in the market, which is why it makes good sense to grow your own. If you've never seen one, you'd be surprised how large they can get (both the berries and the thorny bushes). Their leaves are distinctively frilled, and the berries are as juicy as grapes, and almost translucent. They are delicious in cakes, tarts, compotes, and the quintessentially British dessert, gooseberry fool.

❼ Huckleberries Because huckleberries (also known as bilberries) are understory forest plants, they grow best in shady areas where not much else will thrive—though they do need *some* sun (ideally in the morning) to fruit. Although closely related to blueberries, they have smaller berries and leaves, and a looser branching form. Huckleberries pair beautifully with ferns and evergreen coniferous trees, like redwood or fir. I like to plant them on either side of meandering pathways, for easy foraging.

❽ Raspberries Imagine plucking fresh, fragile raspberries straight from the bush and plopping them into your morning bowl of yogurt and granola. That daydream can easily become reality, as long as you can find space for raspberry plants to get established and stay contained. For the best results, grow raspberries in their own raised bed, with a T-shaped trellis made of metal or wood. The berries can grow almost as well along fence lines or walls with cable trellising, if you prefer. There are technically two types of raspberries: fall-bearing (which fruit on first-year primocanes) and summer-bearing (which fruit on

second-year floricanes). For the easiest maintenance, I tend to stick to primocane varieties so that I can simply prune all the canes down to the ground each fall. If you don't mind a little extra work, however, you can enjoy two harvest seasons (summer and fall) by selectively pruning fall-bearing varieties in the same manner as summer-bearing varieties.

❾ Strawberries While I usually opt to plant strawberries along the edges of raised beds for easy harvesting and maintenance, they can perform just as well planted in the ground, in ornamental beds. I am particularly fond of their large, pretty, three-lobed leaves, which add a welcome contrast to finer-leaved ornamental ground covers. Their delicate white and yellow flowers last for months on end. I recommend looking for everbearing varieties (meaning they will keep producing over a longer period, ideally from spring through summer). My favorites are 'Seascape' (pictured on the previous page) and 'Albion'. For a more concentrated harvest window (for making jam, perhaps), choose a June-bearing variety, like 'Chandler'.

Fruit Trees

The kings and queens of edible perennials, fruit trees are a considerable investment of time and space, but they offer great rewards for relatively little ongoing maintenance. Besides, planting fruit trees is an act of hope, faith, and generosity that connects us to future generations (as well as to their storied past). Choosing the right tree for your property requires the same due diligence as any other plant: Assess the space, sunlight, and climate to find the best match (there's almost always a good tree for your site).

When deciding where to plant fruit trees, be mindful of the harvest (fruit drop) zone within access areas like driveways. Some varieties of fruit trees, including mulberries and plums, are bigger culprits than others. The ideal location is in a wide planting bed, or near other softscape features, like lawns and meadows. Try to keep fruit trees close enough to pathways to ensure ease of access and so that you'll notice when they are ready to harvest.

---

❶ Apples An apple tree is an entry-level option for any garden, with an array of varieties to suit any site. Some apple trees are self-fertilizing, while others need a mate to cross-pollinate. With a deep bench to choose from, your harvesttime can extend from July to November with the right mix of varieties. Apple trees can be pruned back hard to a simple branching structure, which is a great option for smaller spaces or to espalier. (As a bonus, when the trees are kept small, the fruit is easier to pick.) Apples keep exceptionally well when stored properly and are prized for their many culinary possibilities, raw or cooked. You can also use the branch clippings to flavor dishes cooked in a smoker. If I had to choose only one apple variety to plant, it would be 'Fuji' (pictured), a self-fertilizing, easy-to-grow,

sweet stalwart. It can also be fun to experiment with heirloom varieties, like the striking 'Niedzwetzkyana' apple pictured on page 239.

❷ Citrus I could probably write a whole book, or at least an entire chapter, on citrus, but given that these trees will thrive only in specific climate zones, I will restrain myself to a short summary: Sweet or sour—the choice begins there. Lemons and limes (pictured: 'Bearss' lime) can cope with less sun and cooler temperatures than the sweeter oranges, mandarins, and tangelos. Suited to both planters and in-ground planting, citrus are among the most versatile edible garden trees; if you plan it right, you can include a range of varieties that ensures citrus fruit nearly all year round in your garden. Even when they're not in bloom, these evergreen edibles

can be used as specimen focal trees, bushes in borders, accents in pots, and espaliered hedges. In climates with cold winters, potted citrus can be moved into greenhouses to protect them.

❸ Figs With their large, palmlike leaves, fig trees work well in a variety of landscapes. Though you will have the most bountiful harvest if you plant them in full sun, you can still get a decent return in partial sun. In hotter climates the trees can fruit twice, in early and late summer. Even though figs love water, they can thrive with much less than other fruit trees. Ripe fresh figs can be picked straight off the tree and eaten out of hand, or brought inside and served in salads, on cheese boards, or in any number of desserts; dried figs are fantastic as year-round snacks or baked into cookies and other sweet treats.

❹ Loquat A few distinct characteristics make the loquat tree a great option to keep in your back pocket for planting in unconventional locations. To start, this evergreen can get impressively large, with dark, oversize leaves that come in handy for screening fences or providing shade. Second, it can handle partial shade, unlike most fruit trees, making it possible to grow food in otherwise unproductive corners. Lastly, it produces reliably heavy harvests. The only difficulty is figuring out what to make with all the fruit. Jam, drinks, cake, chutney, and even curry are all good bets! Note: These are frost tender.

❺ Mulberries 'Pakistan' mulberries (pictured on the previous page) are my favorite variety, for their berries (which are much larger and more flavorful than most other mulberries) as well as for the way they stand out in the landscape. With their large leaves, they make excellent shade trees, too. Soft, tree-grown berries like these can be a little trickier to harvest than bush berries; the process is primarily done with the old "shake until they drop" technique. (Pro tips: Placing a sheet below the branches makes life easier. And be sure to plant these trees away from furniture and hardscape areas, to minimize staining.)

❻ Pears True orchard trees, pears grow well in fields with other fruiting trees, either their own type or other varieties. They also make a beautiful, stand-alone specimen, and are similar in habit to apples (their botanical cousin), with marginally fewer options to choose from. Pear trees are prone to a deadly disease called fire blight, so it's worth seeking out resistant varieties, like 'Seckel' and 'Warren'. I am deeply fond of the lovely craggy, textured bark of the older trees, which always catch my eye in the landscape.

❼ Persimmons The quintessential edible ornamental specimen, the persimmon offers up gifts through all seasons: pretty buds in spring, lush green leaves in summer as the pollinated flowers start to swell, stunning autumn colors, and cheerful orange bauble-like fruits just in time for the holiday season. Honestly, it's hard not to fall head over heels with the hearty foliage and ribbed bark of this tree. I try to find a place for one in each project, space and light permitting (at least 12 feet/3.5 m for the canopy, and eight or more hours of sun). See if you can find one of the good native varieties available, depending on your region; otherwise, 'Fuyu' and 'Hachiya' are the most commonly available cultivars. 'Fuyu' can be eaten in its natural state, whereas 'Hachiya' is best preserved by drying or freezing and turning into ice cream.

❽ Plums/Pluots Prolific and hardy, these fast-growing stone fruits can tolerate partial shade, and offer a beautiful spring bloom. As they have a relatively brief fruiting season and a shorter shelf life, you'll want to preserve your harvest. Jams, sauces, and even ketchup are great ways to extend the bounty. Make sure to plant these trees outside the "drop zone" of hardscape surfaces; plum "rain" can be a nuisance that you don't want all over a new terrace.

❾ Quinces The quince is among the world's oldest fruit trees. I like them for their hardiness and versatility; the trees thrive in a wide range of climates. Grown in their natural state as either a small tree or bush, quinces can also be espaliered (see page 46) and trained to cover walls or fences. In spring, the branches and flowers are wonderful in arrangements; the fruits are not generally eaten out of hand but are delicious when used to make a paste known as membrillo, a must on any cheese board.

Plant Index

The lists that follow include my favorite edibles for planting outside the vegetable bed. If you don't already know your USDA climate zone, go to planthardiness.ars.usda.gov for more information on which plants will be successful in your specific region. Note that the tender perennials category refers to plants that need to be cut back in winter.

KEY

Size	Sun Requirements
Small Under 2.5 ft (0.75 m); trees up to 9 ft (2.75 m)	Full Sun ○
Medium 2.5–6 ft (0.75–1.8 m); trees 9–20 ft (2.75–6 m)	Partial Shade ◐
Large Over 6 ft (1.8 m); trees over 20 ft (6 m)	Shade Tolerant ●

Edible Ground Covers

Common Name	Harvest Season				Zones	Size	Sun Requirements	Favorite Types or Varietals (if applicable)
	Spring	Summer	Fall	Winter				
Alpine strawberry (*fraises des bois*)	✓				5–8	Small	● ◐ ○	'Yellow Wonder', Alexandria
Lingonberry		✓			2–7	Small	◐ ○	European and Asian
Marjoram	✓	✓	✓		6–9	Small	◐ ○	sweet marjoram, 'Zaatar'
Oregano		✓	✓		5–10	Small	◐ ○	'Compactum', French, Greek, Italian
Rosemary, creeping/trailing	✓	✓	✓	✓	8–10	Small	○	'Huntington Carpet', 'Renzels' (sold as Irene)
Sage		✓	✓		5–10	Small	○	'Berggarten', golden, purple, 'Tricolor'
Strawberry	✓	✓			5–9	Small	◐ ○	'Albion', everbearing, 'Seascape'
Thyme	✓	✓	✓		5–10	Small	◐ ○	English, French, lemon, silver
Wild strawberry		✓			5–9	Small	● ◐	Virginia
Yerba buena	✓	✓	✓		5–10	Small	● ◐	

Tender Perennials

Common Name	Harvest Season				Zones	Size	Sun Requirements	Favorite Types or Varietals (if applicable)
	Spring	Summer	Fall	Winter				
Artichoke	■	■			9–11	Medium	○	'Colorado Star', 'Emerald', 'Green Globe', 'Imperial Star', 'Purple Italian', 'Violetto'
Banana	■	■	■	■	7–11	Large	○	'Ice Cream'
Cardamom			■	■	10–12	Medium	○	Malabar
Chive		■	■		3–9	Small	◐ ○	Garlic, onion
Fiddlehead	■				2–8	Medium	● ◐	Ostrich fern
Ginger	■				8–12	Medium	◐ ○	'Buffalo',
Lemongrass	■	■	■		9–11	Small	○	West Indian
Papaya		■	■		9–11	Large	○	'Maradol', 'Solo'
Rhubarb	■				3–8	Medium	◐ ○	'Crimson Red', 'Prince Albert', 'Victoria'
Roselle hibiscus			■		8–11	Medium	○	
Salmonberry	■				5–9	Medium	● ◐ ○	
Sorrel	■	■	■		3–9	Small	◐ ○	French, red-veined
Stevia		■			9–11	Small	◐ ○	
Thimbleberry	■				3–10	Medium	● ◐	
Turmeric			■	■	8–11	Medium	◐ ○	'Hawaiian Red', 'Indira Yellow'

Woody Perennials

Common Name	Harvest Season				Zones	Size	Sun Requirements	Favorite Types or Varietals (if applicable)
	Spring	Summer	Fall	Winter				
Bamboo	■				6–10	Large	◐ ○	'Red Margin', sweetshoot
Bay laurel (sweet bay)	■	■	■	■	8–10	Medium-large	◐ ○	'MonRik' (sold as Little Ragu)
Blueberry, lowbush		■			2–7	Medium	◐ ○	'FLX-2' (sold as Bountiful Blue), 'Sunshine Blue'
Blueberry, northern highbush		■			4–8	Medium	◐ ○	'Bluecrop', 'Legacy'
Blueberry, southern highbush		■			6–10	Medium	◐ ○	'O'Neal', 'Sentinel', 'Sharpblue'
Chilean guava		■	■		8–11	Medium	○	'Flambeau'
Chokeberry		■	■		3–8	Medium	● ◐ ○	'Brilliantissima', 'Erecta'
Fruiting currants		■			3–8	Medium	◐ ○	Black, red, white
Goji berry		■			5–9	Medium	○	'Crimson Star', 'SMNDSL' (sold as Sweet Lifeberry)

	Harvest Season				Zones	Size	Sun Requirements	Favorite Types or Varietals (if applicable)
Common Name	*Spring*	*Summer*	*Fall*	*Winter*				
Woody Perennials								
Gooseberry		■			4–8	Medium	◐ ○	'Leveller', 'Pax', 'Whinham's Industry', 'Whitesmith'
Highbush cranberry		■			2–7	Large	● ◐ ○	'Andrews', 'Hahs', 'Wentworth'
Huckleberry		■	■		3–9	Medium	● ◐ ○	Evergreen
Jostaberry		■			4–8	Medium	◐ ○	
Lemon verbena		■			8–10	Medium	◐ ○	
Oregon grape		■			5–9	Large	● ◐ ○	
Pineapple guava			■		8–11	Large	○	'Coolidge', 'Nazemata', 'Tharfiona' (sold as Bambina)
Prickly pear			■		7–10	Large	○	Barbary fig, thornless, wheel cactus
Rose	■	■	■		4–10	Medium-large	◐ ○	'Blanc Double de Coubert', 'Cécile Brünner'
Rosemary, upright	■	■	■	■	8–10	Medium	◐ ○	'Barbeque', 'Tuscan Blue'
Serviceberry		■			4–9	Large	● ◐ ○	'Northline', 'Smokey', 'Thiessen'
Tea plant (*Camellia sinensis*)	■	■	■		7–9	Medium	◐	

	Harvest Season				Zones	Size	Sun Requirements	Favorite Types or Varietals (if applicable)
Vines								
Blackberry		■			4–9	Large	◐ ○	'Navaho', Prime-Ark series, 'Triple Crown'
Boysenberry		■			5–10	Medium	◐ ○	
Dragon fruit		■	■		9–11	Large	○	'Physical Graffiti', 'S-8', 'Valdivia Roja'
Grape			■		4–10	Large	◐ ○	'Concord', 'Flame Seedless', 'Thompson Seedless'
Hops		■			4–9	Large	○	'Cascade', 'Centennial'
Kiwifruit			■		5–10	Large	○	'Hayward', 'Vincent'
Loganberry		■			5–10	Medium	◐ ○	'LY654'
Marionberry		■			6–9	Medium	◐ ○	
Passion fruit (granadilla)		■	■		9–11	Large	◐ ○	'Possum Purple', 'Red Rover'
Raspberry		■			3–10	Medium-large	◐ ○	'Fallgold', 'Heritage', 'Jewel'
Tayberry		■			5–10	Medium	◐ ○	'Buckingham', 'Medana'

Common Name	Harvest Season				Zones	Size	Sun Requirements	Favorite Types or Varietals (if applicable)
	Spring	Summer	Fall	Winter				
CITRUS								
Australian finger lime	■			■	9–11	Medium	○	'Red Champagne'
Grapefruit	■			■	9–11	Medium	◐ ○	'Oroblanco', 'Ruby Red'
Kumquat	■			■	9–11	Small–Medium	◐ ○	'Centennial Variegated', 'Nagami'
Lemon	■			■	8–11	Medium	◐ ○	'Eureka', 'Eureka Variegated Pink' (sold as Pink Lemonade), Meyer
Lime	■			■	8–11	Medium	○	'Bearss', Key/Mexican, makrut (use leaf)
Mandarin (tangerine)	■			■	9–11	Medium	○	
Orange	■			■	9–11	Medium	○	'Cara Cara' navel, 'Trovita', 'Moro' blood
Pomelo	■			■	9–11	Medium	○	'Chandler', 'Kao Pan', Tahitian
Satsuma	■				9-11	Medium	○	'Owari'
Tangelo	■			■	9–11	Medium	○	'Minneola', 'Orlando'
FRUIT								
Apple		■			3–9	Medium	○	'Fuji', 'Honeycrisp', 'Pink Lady'
Apricot		■			4–9	Medium	○	'Blenheim', 'Harcot'
Asian pear		■	■		5–9	Medium	○	'Shinseiki', 'Twentieth Century'
Avocado				■	8–11	Large	○	'Bacon', 'Fuerte', 'Hass'
Cherry		■			5–9	Medium	○	'Bing', 'Stella'
Elderberry		■			4–9	Large	◐ ○	'Johns', 'Nova', 'York'
Fig		■			7–10	Large	◐ ○	'Kadota', 'Mission'
Guava		■			9–11	Large	○	Strawberry guava
Loquat	■				7–10	Large	◐ ○	'Benlehr', 'Champagne', 'Gold Nugget'
Mango		■			10–11	Large	○	'Carabao', 'Keitt'
Mulberry		■			5–9	Large	○	Black, 'Pakistan'
Mulberry, weeping		■			5–9	Small	◐ ○	
Nectarine		■			5–9	Medium	○	'Arctic Queen', 'Double Delight'
Olive			■		8–10	Medium	○	'Manzanilla', 'Mission'
Pawpaw		■			5–8	Large	● ◐ ○	'Pennsylvania Golden', 'Prolific', 'Shenandoah'

Trees

Common Name	Harvest Season°				Zones	Size	Sun Requirements	Favorite Types or Varietals (if applicable)
	Spring	Summer	Fall	Winter				
Peach		▦			5–9	Medium	○	'Arctic Supreme', 'Babcock'
Pear		▦	▦		4–9	Medium	○	'Doyenné du Comice', 'Red Sensation Bartlett'
Persimmon			▦		4–9	Medium	○	'Fuyu', 'Hachiya', 'Maru' chocolate
Plum		▦			4–9	Medium	◐ ○	'Santa Rosa'
Pluot		▦			6–9	Medium	○	'Dapple Dandy', 'Flavor King'
Pomegranate			▦		8–11	Medium	○	'Wonderful'
Quince			▦		4–9	Medium	◐ ○	'Serbian Gold', 'Smyrna'
NUT								
Almond			▦		6–9	Large	○	'All-in-One', 'Nonpareil'
Chestnut			▦		4–9	Large	○	'AU Buck' series, 'Dunstan'
Hazelnut			▦		4–9	Large	◐ ○	'Dorris', 'Wepster'
Macadamia	▦	▦	▦		9–11	Large	○	'Beaumont'
Pecan			▦		5–9	Large	○	'Amling', 'Mahan', 'Stuart'
Pistachio			▦		7–11	Large	○	'Famosa', 'Kerman'
Walnut			▦		4–9	Large	○	Black
SUBTROPIC								
Allspice			▦		10–12	Large	○	
Breadfruit		▦	▦		9–11	Large	○	'Ma'afala'
Carob			▦		9–11	Large	○	
Cherimoya	▦			▦	10	Large	◐ ○	'Orton', 'Pierce'
Cocoa	▦			▦	11–13	Large	◐ ○	Criollo, Forastero, Trinitario
Coconut	▦	▦	▦	▦	10–12	Large	○	'Jamaican Tall'
Curry leaf tree (small tree)		▦	▦		9–12	Medium	○	
Custard apple	▦			▦	9–11	Large	○	'San Pablo', 'Tikai'
Date palm			▦		9–12	Large	○	'Barhi', 'Medjool'
Jaboticaba	▦				9–11	Large	○	'Grimal', 'Sabara'
Jackfruit		▦	▦		9–12	Large	○	'Bangkok Lemon', 'Dang Surya', 'Excalibur Red', 'Mai 1'
Sapote		▦			10–12	Large	○	
Star fruit	▦	▦	▦		9–11	Large	○	'Arkin', 'Fwang Tung', 'Kari', Sri Kembangan
Tamarind	▦				10–11	Large	○	

Resources

Advice and Inspiration

The American Horticultural Society A–Z Encyclopedia of Garden Plants
by Christopher Brickell

Annie's Annuals
anniesannuals.com

Calflora Plant Database
calflora.org

Dave Wilson
davewilson.com

Epic Gardening
epicgardening.com

Local University Extension Programs

Monty Don
montydon.com

Monrovia
monrovia.com

Native Plants Database
wildflower.org/plants

Native Plant Trust Plant Finder
plantfinder.nativeplanttrust.org

North American Native Plant Society
nanps.org

Phone a Farmer
thebackyardfarmcompany.com

Rodale Institute
rodaleinstitute.org

Ron Finley
ronfinley.com

Sarah Raven
sarahraven.com

Stone Barns Center
stonebarnscenter.org/farm

Time-Saver Standards for Landscape Architecture
by Charles Harris and Nicholas Dines

University of California Integrated Pest Management
ipm.ucanr.edu/index.html

Master Gardener Program
ahsgardening.org/gardening -resources/master-gardeners

USDA
planthardiness.ars.usda.gov

The New Sunset Western Garden Book
by the editors of *Sunset* magazine

Classes

The Backyard Farm Company
thebackyardfarmcompany.com /online-gardening-courses

4-H
4-h.org

Occidental Arts & Ecology Center
oaec.org

Soil Food Web
soilfoodweb.com

Garden Accessories

Duluth Trading Co.
duluthtrading.com

Etsy
etsy.com

Gardeners.com
gardeners.com

Heartwood Homestead
theheartwoodhomestead.com

Hort and Pott
hortandpott.com

Master Garden products
mastergardenproducts.com

Seattle Urban Farm Company
seattleurbanfarmco.com

Terrain
shopterrain.com

Williams Sonoma
williams-sonoma.com

Pots and Planters

CB2
cb2.com

Grassroots Fabric Pots
grassrootsfabricpots.com

Vego Garden
vegogarden.com

Seed Companies

Baker Creek
rareseeds.com

Fedco
fedcoseeds.com

High Mowing Seed Company
highmowingseeds.com

Johnny's Selected Seeds
johnnyseeds.com

Grow Organic
groworganic.com

Renee's Garden
reneesgarden.com

Row 7
row7seeds.com

Seed Sharing
exchange.seedsavers.org

Territorial
territorialseed.com

Soil Health

A&L Western Ag Labs
al-labs-west.com

The Backyard Farm Company
thebackyardfarmcompany.com

Bio365
bio365.com

Down to Earth
downtoearthfertilizer.com

EB Stone
ebstone.org

TerraVesco
terravesco.com

Vital Garden Supply
vitalgardensupply.com

Tools

Barebones
barebonesliving.com

Felco
felco.com

Niwaki
niwaki.com

Opinel
opinel-usa.com

Victorinox
victorinox.com

Acknowledgments

Thank you to every individual who played a part, big or small, in making this book a reality. Your contributions have made it a true labor of love, and I am forever grateful to you all.

To the visionary, Bridget Monroe Itkin. Your editorial excellence and guidance have been a gift. This book wouldn't exist without you.

Deepest gratitude to my core dream team. Your fingerprints shape every page. From wordsmithing to wide angles, you've put so much intention and thought into every inch. Thank you for sharing your talents. You have all taught me so much. Christiana Drewry, you have been integral to the creation of this book. Your many words, pictures, and farming wisdom permeate so perfectly throughout these pages. Your contributions have been invaluable to me and the success of this book. I am blessed to work with you each day. Ellen Morrissey, I am so thankful for your mentorship, editorial mastery, and friendship throughout this journey. Your endless support and exquisite words have helped create something truly special. Sasha Gulish, our creative director in chief: Seeing the world through your lens is the most beautiful thing. Thank you for always bringing your bright light and big ideas to the table.

To Tyler and Tolan Florence for your contribution, friendship, and the projects we continue to hatch together. To friend and amazing designer Susan Skornicka, the creator of the glorious edible woodland covered planters. To Gary Graw for your rooftop farm vision and Kelly Lauber for the vegetable bouquet inspiration. And to photographers Kodiak Drewry, Adam Potts, Caitlin Atkinson, and all those who contributed time and effort to the countless photo shoots.

To all of our wonderful clients, the heartbeat of this book. Thank you for sharing your gardens with us, and for your willingness to explore the opportunities of growing food close to home. You are constant inspiration and motivation to me.

A huge thank-you to the team at Artisan—including Lia Ronnen, Zach Greenwald, Suet Chong, Jane Treuhaft, Toni Tajima, Hillary Leary, Paula Brisco, Elissa Santos, Abby Knudsen, Nancy Murray, Allison McGeehon, Brittany Dennison, and Abigail Solinsky—for bringing our mission to life and riding the waves so gracefully to produce this beautiful book with me. With special thanks as well to Rodrigo and Anna Corral for the wonderful jacket design and friendship.

To the incredible team that has designed and grown these gardens—my design partner, Christian Macke; Olivia Miller; Cole Skaggs; Amy Rice-Jones; and Rebecca Chasin. I am so grateful to each and every one of you for showing up each day and bringing creativity and joy to all that we do. And to all of the craftspeople that turn our ideas into form: Thank you for all of the dedication, care, and attention over the years, and for the countless hours putting up with my "bright" ideas. You all deserve a medal.

To Nicole Balin for your vision, guidance, and shaping the stories we tell. For always being right there whenever I call on you for support.

To Popsy Douglas for sharing your wisdom, support, and laughter through this journey. Here's to many more treasured "who has the biggest harvest" cross-pond calls. Mrs. "Tiggywinkle" Douglas, I promise never to pronounce herb "erb."

Bonnie and Rosie, you are the bedrock from which all of this has been built. Your support, love, and muddy paw prints are immeasurable. You are my world.

Index

Photography Credits

Photographs by Sasha Gulish, except for the following:

Adam Potts: pages 27 (*top*), 41, and 42–43

Caitlin Atkinson: page 91

Christian Douglas: pages 10, 31 (*top left, bottom left and right*); 45; 72–73; 78 (*top*); 83 (*bottom right*); 87 (*bottom right*); 90 (*bottom right*); 97; 112; 118; 122; 150–151; 152 (*right*); 153 (*right*); 173; 177; 178; 179; 192; 197; 212–213; 215 (*top left, middle right, bottom row*); 219; 221 (*top right, middle right, bottom middle and right*); 225 (*top left*); 227 (*top middle and right, center, middle right*); 229 (*top left and middle, middle left, center, bottom row*); 231; 233 (*top middle, middle left, bottom left and right*); 235; 237 (*center, bottom right*); and 239

Kodiak Drewry: pages 47 (*top right*) 80–81, 84–85, 126–127, 136–137, and 138–139

Courtesy of Shutterstock: page 223: (*middle left*) Nahhana; (*center*) Marie Shark; (*bottom middle*) Bowonpat Sakaew; (*bottom right*) Rattana; page 225: (*middle left*) Jaclyn Vernace; (*bottom left*) Nelly Filimonova, (*bottom middle*) Rose Marinelli; page 233: (*middle left*) Alex Coan; (*center*) David Barratt; (*bottom middle*) Vlad Siaber; and page 237: (*middle left*) traction

About the Author

CHRISTIAN DOUGLAS is an award-winning landscape designer and the founder of Christian Douglas Design, which creates extraordinary culinary gardens, and the Backyard Farm Company, where he and his team of professional farmers teach homeowners around the world how to grow food. Christian was awarded the California Home+Design Award for landscape design and has been featured in the *Wall Street Journal*, *Architectural Digest*, *California Home+Design*, *Sunset*, and other major publications.

About the Contributors

SASHA GULISH is a photographer/director based in the San Francisco Bay Area. Since studying art at UC Berkeley, Sasha has worked in the advertising and editorial industry for over two decades, both in the US and internationally. Her primary focus lies in capturing products, people, and places, continually drawing inspiration from the intrinsic beauty of the natural world and the deep human connections it creates.

ELLEN MORRISSEY is a writer, editor, and project manager who collaborates with authors and publishers to produce illustrated books on a range of lifestyle topics, including cooking and entertaining, home design, gardening, health and wellness, crafts, and more. For many years, she was Editorial Director of Books and Special Projects for Martha Stewart, and prior to that, she edited cookbooks at Condé Nast and HarperCollins.

CHRISTIANA DREWRY is a farmer, writer, and landscape designer. She has led the Backyard Farm Company since 2019, managing edible landscapes throughout Northern California and educating home gardeners around the world. Christiana studied literature and community agriculture and has always seen the beauty in being close to your food source. She has grown food for nonprofits, three-Michelin-star restaurants, schoolyards, and small-scale organic farms from Scotland to Nicaragua.